ALASKA
Hiking Guide
2025 - 2026

Your Essential Companion for Trekking Routes, Trail Insights/Safety & Travel Planning

Colin Phan

Disclaimer

The information presented in This Hiking Guide 2025 - 2026 is intended to provide accurate and up-to-date details about hiking trails, permits, campsites, and other essential aspects of exploring this location. Every effort has been made to ensure the reliability of the content at the time of publication; however, conditions, regulations, and policies are subject to change without notice.

Hikers are strongly encouraged to verify trail conditions, permit requirements, weather forecasts, and safety guidelines with official sources and local authorities before embarking on their journey. The authors and publishers assume no responsibility for any inaccuracies, omissions, or changes that may occur after publication.

Outdoor activities involve inherent risks, including but not limited to sudden weather changes, wildlife encounters, physical injury, and navigation challenges. Readers are responsible for their safety and should exercise caution, proper planning, and sound judgment while exploring. By using this guide, readers acknowledge and accept these risks.

This publication is for informational purposes only and does not substitute professional advice or official park regulations.

Table of Contents

Chapter 1

Introduction to Alaska's Hiking

1.1. Why Hike in Alaska

Alaska is a hiker's dream, offering some of the world's most diverse and awe-inspiring landscapes. From towering mountain ranges to sprawling glaciers, Alaska's hiking destinations provide an unparalleled connection to nature. The state's vastness means you can find solitude in places where few others have set foot, making it an ideal destination for those seeking adventure, tranquility, or a challenge. Why Hike in Alaska? First, it's the sheer variety of terrain you'll encounter. Alaska has it all if you want to trek through wildflower meadows, climb rocky peaks, or walk along pristine coastlines. Second, Alaska's wildlife makes the experience unique.

Hiking here offers the chance to see animals like grizzly bears, moose, and eagles in their natural habitats. Finally, there's the weather. While it can be unpredictable, the light during summer – especially the long days – offers extraordinary opportunities for exploration. The summer months provide nearly endless daylight, and in the winter, many trails offer a serene, snow-covered landscape perfect for cross-country skiing or snowshoeing. Alaska is not for the casual hiker. Its rugged trails demand respect and preparation.

1.2. The Beauty and Diversity of Alaska's Trails

Alaska's trails are as varied as its landscapes, and this diversity is what makes hiking here so appealing to adventurers of all kinds. From the lush forests of the southeastern coast to the icy wilderness of the interior, Alaska offers a range of hiking experiences that can cater to every skill level. In the south, the Kenai Peninsula provides accessible trails with views of glaciers, rivers, and coastal cliffs. The popular Harding Icefield Trail in Kenai Fjords National Park gives hikers the chance to look out over expansive glaciers that meet rocky terrain. If you venture further north, the challenging Denali National Park offers its most famous trail, the Savage River Loop, providing hikers with panoramic views of the majestic Denali Peak, North America's highest mountain. The interior of the state, including Wrangell-St. Elias National Park is a vast wilderness that stretches over 13 million acres. Here, you can hike along glaciers, across rivers, or explore the pristine beauty of remote terrain where few people venture.

Further southeast, the Tongass National Forest in the rainforests of Alaska's Panhandle boasts a different kind of hiking experience with its wet, moss-laden forests and dramatic coastal views. In Alaska, no two trails are alike, and each offers its own set of challenges and rewards. Whether you are exploring dense forests, tundra landscapes, or rugged mountain peaks, there is no shortage of beauty to behold.

1.3. What Makes Alaska Unique for Hiking

What sets Alaska apart from other hiking destinations is its combination of wilderness, solitude, and raw, untamed nature. Alaska is home to vast stretches of wild terrain that remain largely untouched by human development. Many trails are in remote areas, meaning hikers can experience unspoiled landscapes, sometimes for miles, without encountering anyone else. One unique aspect of hiking in Alaska is the chance to witness the changing seasons in extreme ways. In the summer, the days are long—sometimes lasting for 24 hours in the far northern regions—allowing you to experience the outdoors at all hours of the day.

During the fall, the tundra turns vibrant shades of red and gold, creating a spectacular display of color. In winter, the trails take on a quiet, peaceful atmosphere with snowy landscapes perfect for cross-country skiing and snowshoeing. Alaska's wildlife is another defining feature of the hiking experience. Bears, moose, wolves, caribou, and countless other species can be spotted while hiking, giving visitors a rare opportunity to observe animals in their natural habitats. For many hikers, seeing wildlife up close is one of the highlights of an Alaskan adventure. Finally, Alaska's glaciers and mountains provide a backdrop that is unlike anything you'll find elsewhere. These towering peaks and ancient ice fields offer unparalleled views, making every step of the hike feel like a journey through a living, breathing wilderness.

Chapter 2

Plan Your Alaska Hiking Adventure

2.1. Best Time to Hike in Alaska.

Because of Alaska's vast and varied landscape, the best time to hike varies depending on the region and type of hiking experience desired. While the state provides incredible hiking opportunities all year, the majority of visitors come during the summer months, when trails are more accessible and the weather is most pleasant.

Summer (June–August): The Peak Hiking Season

The summer months, from June to August, are the most popular for hiking in Alaska, and with good reason. During this time, the state's weather is at its most manageable, and the days are long—especially in the northern regions, where daylight lasts nearly 24 hours during the height of summer. Hikers can make the most of their time on the trail with this extended daylight, which allows for longer hikes and more daylight hours for exploration.

Southern Alaska, including Kenai Fjords National Park and Kachemak Bay, has warmer temperatures, ranging from 50°F to 70°F (10°C to 21°C), though higher elevations may still experience cooler conditions. Temperatures in northern areas, such as Denali National Park, range from 40°F to 60°F (4°C to 16°C), making hiking more comfortable. However, even in the summer, conditions can change quickly, so hikers should always be prepared for rain, wind, or cooler temperatures, particularly in the mountains and at higher elevations.

Summer is also the season when Alaska's iconic wildlife is most active. Along the trails, you are likely to see moose, bears, caribou, and a variety of bird species. This season is ideal for viewing wildlife in their natural habitats because there is plenty of food, and warmer weather brings animals out into the open. However, it also means that you should be cautious in your encounters, particularly with bears, and always take safety precautions, such as carrying bear spray and making noise on the trail.

This is also the time when the majority of Alaska's popular hiking trails are completely accessible. Trails that are typically blocked by snow or difficult conditions in other seasons are clear of obstacles, allowing hikers to reach remote areas more easily. Popular hikes, such as the Harding Icefield Trail in Kenai Fjords National Park and the Kesugi Ridge Trail in Denali State Park, are best experienced during the summer months.

Fall (September- October): A More Relaxing Experience. Fall in Alaska, from September to October, is an underappreciated but breathtaking time to hike. The weather can still be relatively mild in early September, but temperatures drop as the month progresses. In September, highs may range from 40°F to 60°F (4°C to 16°C), but by October, temperatures will have dropped significantly, and the first signs of winter will be visible, with highs ranging from 20°F to 40°F (-6°C to 4°C).

Fall in Alaska also marks a remarkable transformation of the landscape, with the tundra and forests changing to vibrant shades of red, yellow, and gold. Many of Alaska's plants, such as blueberries, are at their peak during this time, and the landscape becomes stunningly colorful, making it a photographer's dream. Rain and early snow can cause some paths to become muddy or slippery, making trail conditions slightly less predictable. However, with fewer visitors in the fall, hikers looking for a peaceful experience will find quieter trails and more solitude.

Wildlife in the fall is preparing for winter, so while sightings are still common, animals such as bears are more focused on feeding and hibernation. Hiking during this time provides an excellent opportunity to observe animals gathering food and displaying interesting seasonal behaviors.

Winter (November-March): For Adventurous Hikers
Winter hiking in Alaska, from November to March, is only for the most adventurous and prepared hikers. Alaska's winters are particularly cold and harsh. Especially in the northern parts of the state, where

temperatures can drop below 0°F (-18°C). The majority of the trails are covered in snow, so hiking during this time is often combined with cross-country skiing, snowshoeing, or winter camping.

Winter daylight hours are significantly shorter, with some areas receiving only a few hours of light per day, particularly in the north. This makes winter hiking a unique challenge because hikers must be more strategic with their timing and equipment. Trail conditions can be icy and snowy, so traction devices such as crampons or microspikes are essential, as is layering for warmth.

Nonetheless, winter hiking provides a unique opportunity to experience Alaska's snowy wilderness in a way that few others do. The peaceful stillness of the snow-covered landscape is extremely tranquil, and the possibility of seeing the Northern Lights (Aurora Borealis) while hiking makes this time of year truly magical for the right adventurer. Some of Alaska's most popular trails, including those in Denali National Park, have winter access, and guided snowshoeing or skiing tours can help you navigate the wilderness in these harsh conditions.

Spring (April- May): A Time for Early Hiking.

Spring in Alaska, from April to May, is the transition from winter to summer, and the weather can be unpredictable. While lower elevations begin to thaw and become more accessible, higher elevation trails remain snow-covered, making spring a transitional season for hiking. Daytime temperatures can range from 20°F to 50°F (-6°C to 10°C), and spring rain is common, particularly along coastlines.

Spring is ideal for early-season hiking in southern Alaska, particularly in Ketchikan and Anchorage, where the snow has melted, and the trails are relatively dry. Wildflowers begin to bloom in late May, and the landscape slowly but steadily reawakens. However, higher-altitude hikes, such as those in Denali, will remain inaccessible, so check trail conditions and prepare for changing weather.

2.2. Weather and Climate Considerations.

Alaska's weather is well-known for being unpredictable, with drastic changes occurring even within a single day. Understanding the climate and weather patterns before embarking on a hiking trip is critical for ensuring safety and preparedness. This section will look at Alaska's weather and climate, focusing on how to plan and prepare for hikes in this harsh environment.

Understanding Alaska's microclimates

Alaska has a vast geographical area, so its climate varies greatly depending on location. Coastal areas, particularly in the southeast, have much milder climates due to the ocean's moderating effect. On the other hand, the interior of the state, including Fairbanks and Denali National Park, has extreme continental climate conditions—hot summers and cold winters. Coastal regions, such as Anchorage or Juneau, have more temperate weather, with temperatures ranging from 40°F to 70°F (4°C to 21°C) in the summer, but they still experience rain, fog, and snow on occasion.

In contrast, the interior of the state, particularly the Alaska Range and Wrangell-St. Elias may experience extreme weather changes. In the summer, these areas can reach temperatures as high as 80°F (27°C), but cold fronts can arrive quickly, causing temperature drops. Winter months in these areas can bring consistent snow, ice, and temperatures well below freezing, often dropping to -40°F (-40°C) or lower.

Alaskan weather can be unpredictable from one hour to the next. A sunny morning can quickly turn to heavy rain, wind, or snow, particularly at higher elevations. Hikers should always be prepared for unexpected weather changes, regardless of the season. This is why layering clothing and planning for all weather conditions is critical.

Rain and Snow: Prepare for Wet Conditions
Rain is common throughout Alaska, especially in the southeast, including Ketchikan and Sitka, where the coastal environment causes frequent precipitation. Even during the summer, hikers are likely to encounter rain, particularly in dense forests or near glaciers. Proper waterproof gear—such as a good rain jacket, boots, and

dry bags—is essential for remaining comfortable and safe in these conditions.

Snowfall is common in Alaska's mountainous terrain, especially at higher elevations. Even during the summer, some trails may remain snow-covered, making trekking more difficult. In the late spring and early fall, snow can accumulate quickly in the mountains, making certain trails less accessible.

Wind and Cold: Prepare for the Chill.
Alaska's rugged terrain also produces strong winds, especially along the coast and at higher elevations. These winds can make the temperature feel much colder than it is, so hikers should be prepared for wind chill factors that can drop well below freezing, even in the middle of summer. When hiking in windy areas, particularly on exposed ridges or near the coast, wear windproof clothing and layer carefully.

Hikers heading into the interior or northern regions must be prepared for cold weather, as temperatures can drop unexpectedly even in the summer. Even if temperatures were relatively warm during the day, they could plummet at night. A well-insulated sleeping bag, warm clothing, and wind-resistant layers will keep you comfortable and safe.

2.3. Packing for an Alaskan Hike.

When planning a hiking trip in Alaska, having the right gear is more than just about comfort; it's about ensuring your safety and preparedness for any challenges that the rugged terrain or unpredictable weather may present. Alaska's wilderness is known for its extremes, so being prepared is essential for getting the most out of your hike. With the right packing strategy, you can concentrate more on the breathtaking scenery and less on the discomfort of being unprepared.

Essential gear for Alaska's trails.

A good hiking experience in Alaska begins with the proper backpack. To carry everything you need for the hike, you'll need a sturdy, comfortable pack. A pack with a capacity of 40-65 liters is ideal for a multiday hike. It should be light enough not to cause strain but strong enough to withstand rough conditions. Look for a backpack with adjustable straps, good padding, and breathable material to keep you comfortable on long treks. You should be able to fit all of your gear, including food, water, and extra layers, without overfilling your pack.

Water is always the priority on any hike, and Alaska is no exception. Depending on the length of the hike and the availability of water sources along the way, you'll need a reliable hydration system. A good water bottle or hydration system, such as a CamelBak, can help you stay hydrated while keeping your pack light. Aim for a capacity of at least 2-3 liters to ensure you have enough for extended periods without access to fresh water.

Another essential item is a headlamp or flashlight. Although Alaska's summer daylight hours are long, the days can shorten unexpectedly, and certain regions may experience low light even during the daytime. If you end up on the trail for longer than expected, you'll need a good headlamp. Pack extra batteries, as cold weather drains battery life faster than usual.

Hiking in Alaska's remote areas requires the use of navigation tools. While some trails are well-marked, others are less developed and necessitate a more thorough approach to avoid getting lost. It's always a good idea to carry a physical, waterproof map of the area you'll be hiking in. A compass can also be useful, especially in areas where trails are not always clear. Furthermore, many hikers now carry GPS devices or download apps on their smartphones, which can be useful but should never replace the fundamental tools of map and compass.

First-aid kits should never be overlooked. Accidents happen, and the Alaskan wilderness is not a place to go unprepared. A well-stocked kit should include bandages, antiseptic wipes, blister treatments, and any personal medications that you may require. Tweezers for removing ticks and splinters are also useful. Carrying an emergency whistle can help you signal for help if you get into a difficult situation.

Trekking poles are another accessory that can improve your hiking experience. They provide stability on rocky or uneven terrain and can relieve strain on your knees when descending steep slopes. Adjustable trekking poles are ideal because they allow you to customize the length based on the terrain or your comfort level. They're also easy to store when not in use.

In Alaska, bear encounters are a reality. While these creatures are not inherently dangerous if left alone, it is critical to have bear spray and understand how to use it. Most hikers carry bear spray in an easily accessible holster, as quick access is critical in a potential encounter. When camping in bear country, always use bear-proof containers and adhere to best food storage practices.

Layering for Variable Weather
One of the most important aspects of packing for Alaska is getting ready for the unpredictable weather. It is not uncommon for hikers to see multiple seasons in one day. Alaska's weather can change from sunny to rainy to snowy in a matter of hours, so layering clothes is essential. Layering allows you to easily add or remove clothing depending on your body temperature and the weather.

The first layer, closest to your skin, is your base layer. The base layer is designed to wick moisture away from your skin, keeping you dry and warm. Merino wool, synthetic fabrics, and silk are all excellent choices for base layers because they allow sweat to evaporate without leaving you damp and cold. Avoid cotton because it absorbs moisture and cools the body. For warmer months, choose a lightweight base layer, while a heavier option is recommended for cooler hikes.

The middle layer serves as insulation. This is the layer that retains body heat. In Alaska, a fleece jacket, a softshell, or a down vest will provide warmth without adding bulk. The mid-layer should be breathable enough to prevent overheating while still providing adequate warmth in cold conditions. If you're hiking in colder weather, go for thicker, insulated jackets. During milder summer days, lighter options are adequate.

The outer layer protects you from wind and snow. Alaska's weather is unpredictable, so bring a windproof and waterproof jacket and pants to protect yourself from the elements. Materials like Gore-Tex and other breathable fabrics are extremely effective because they protect you from wind and rain while allowing moisture to escape, preventing you from becoming overly sweaty. In Alaska, where the weather can change quickly, having a dependable outer layer is essential for comfort.

When layering, don't overlook your extremities. Warm hats and gloves are essential, especially if you're hiking in colder weather or at higher elevations. Wool or synthetic gloves stay warm even when wet. In the warmer months, you may choose a sun hat to protect your face from the sun. Neck gaiters are also a useful piece of gear that can protect your neck and face from the wind, sun, or cold, depending on the weather.

Socks are another essential item that is often overlooked. Wool or synthetic socks are ideal for hiking in Alaska. These materials help to regulate body temperature, keep feet dry, and reduce the risk of blisters. Cotton socks should be avoided because they retain moisture and can cause discomfort or even frostbite in extremely cold weather conditions.

Footwear, Navigation, and Safety Essentials.
The terrain in Alaska can be as varied as the weather, so selecting the appropriate footwear is critical. For the majority of hikes, sturdy, waterproof hiking boots are the best choice. These boots offer ankle support, stability on rocky or uneven terrain, and protection from water and mud. Look for boots that are both durable and comfortable, as Alaska's trails can be long and difficult. To avoid blisters, it is also recommended that you break in your boots before your trip.

In some cases, lighter trail running shoes may be appropriate, particularly on well-kept paths. These shoes are breathable, lightweight, and allow for quick movement, but they may not offer as much protection in harsh environments. If you're going on a short, relatively easy hike in a less remote area, trail running shoes may suffice.

After a long day on the trail, a pair of camp shoes can help your feet relax. Simple sandals or slip-ons are ideal for relaxing at camp after a strenuous hike.

Having dependable navigation tools is also important. As previously stated, maps, compasses, and GPS devices are extremely useful for orienting yourself. You may come across areas with few trail markers, so having a map and compass will help you safely navigate back to your starting point. Downloading trail apps or carrying a handheld GPS device can give you extra peace of mind, but always back up your digital tools with traditional methods because battery life can be unpredictable.

1. Trail Access Permits.
While Alaska's hiking trails are well-known for their accessibility, some areas require permits to help manage visitor numbers, protect the environment, and ensure safety. The need for a permit is determined by the location, the length of the hike, and whether you will be entering protected areas such as national parks, wildlife refuges, or conservation areas.

Backcountry hiking and camping require a permit in many of Alaska's national parks and preserves, including Denali National Park, Wrangell-St. Elias National Park, and Glacier Bay National Park. These permits typically ensure that hikers are prepared for the challenges of the wilderness, and they may include important information about safety, bear activity, trail conditions, and local regulations. Permits for backcountry campsites or longer treks may also be required, which can usually be obtained online or in person at ranger stations. Some areas may have a quota system, which means that only a certain number of people can visit specific areas each day to prevent overuse and protect natural resources.

Permits are typically not required for shorter day hikes unless you are hiking in a highly controlled area. However, it is always best to check with the relevant park or land management agency before heading out to confirm whether permits are required for your preferred trail. For example, when hiking on private property or in state-managed parks, you should check to see if a permit is required for parking, special access, or certain recreational activities.

2. Rules and Regulations to Know.

While Alaska's trails are beautiful, they can also be harsh. To protect both visitors and the land, specific regulations are in place. These rules are intended to preserve ecosystems while minimizing human impact on the environment. The following are the most important rules to be aware of before hitting the trails.

Leave No Trace: Alaska's wilderness is pristine, and maintaining its integrity requires responsible practices. Always follow the "Leave No Trace" principles, which include removing all trash, minimizing campfire impacts, and avoiding the destruction of plants and wildlife. To avoid trampling delicate vegetation, stay on marked trails whenever possible.

Campfire Regulations: While campfires are allowed in some areas, they are prohibited in many others to protect fragile ecosystems. Always check the rules for the trail or park you plan to visit. If campfires are permitted, only use established fire rings and avoid gathering wood from the surrounding forest. In some areas, camp stoves are preferred over campfires for cooking.

Bear Safety: One of Alaska's most important regulations concerns bear safety. Bears are common throughout much of the state, so it's critical to follow all bear safety rules. Never approach a bear, and keep food and scented items in bear-resistant containers or safely hanging from a tree. When hiking, make noise to alert bears to your presence and avoid startling them. It is also advisable to carry bear spray and understand how to use it effectively.

No Dogs on Trails: Dogs are prohibited on many Alaska trails, particularly those in national parks or preserves, to protect wildlife and ensure the safety of both pets and hikers. If dogs are allowed on certain trails, they must be kept on a leash. It is critical to double-check the regulations for the specific trail or area you intend to hike.

Fishing and Hunting Regulations: If you intend to fish or hunt during your hike, you should familiarize yourself with local regulations. Most areas in Alaska require fishing and hunting permits, and some may have strict seasonal restrictions. To avoid potential violations, make sure to research the specific rules for your area.

Alaska's state parks each have their own set of rules. Some parks, for example, require hikers to register their trips before entering the backcountry, whereas others may limit campfires or access to specific areas. Before your trip, always check the regulations with the state park office or their website.

3. Wildlife and Environmental Safety Tips
Alaska's wild and untamed nature supports a diverse range of wildlife, including large mammals such as bears, moose, and bison, as well as smaller creatures such as wolves, foxes, and a wide variety of birds. While these animals are fascinating to watch, they must be treated with respect, and there are specific safety guidelines to follow to reduce your risk and protect the animals.

Bear Safety: Bears are a major concern for hikers in Alaska, particularly in areas with abundant food sources. If you encounter a bear, stay calm, avoid making sudden movements, and slowly back away. Never run from a bear. Bear spray is essential in bear country and should be easily accessible on your hip or pack. If a bear charges, use bear spray as a deterrent. Always store your food away from your tent and sleeping area, and never keep it inside your tent. In some remote areas, you may be required to use a bear-resistant canister to store food.

Moose Safety: Although moose are not aggressive, they can become dangerous if they feel threatened. If you see a moose, keep your distance, especially if it's a mother and her calf. Moose can charge if they feel cornered or threatened, so keep a safe distance and avoid approaching them. They are frequently found near streams, rivers, and areas with dense vegetation.

Insect Protection: Alaska is well-known for its bugs, especially during the warmer months when mosquitos and flies are at their most active. While they may not endanger your life, they can certainly disrupt your comfort. Mosquitoes are particularly abundant in marshy and low-lying areas. To prevent bites, wear long sleeves, pants, and a head net. Insect repellent is also a good idea; choose one with DEET for the best protection. Remember that ticks can be found in some areas, so always check yourself for ticks after hiking.

Wildlife Viewing: Keep a respectful distance from wildlife. Never try to feed wild animals because it can alter their natural behaviors and make them more dangerous. Carry a camera with a telephoto lens to capture close-up shots without getting too close. If you're traveling with a group, stick together and hike in groups, as they're less likely to provoke an animal. Allow a group of animals, such as moose or caribou, to move freely.

Environmental hazards in Alaska's wilderness include avalanches, unstable ice, unpredictable river currents, and extreme weather. Before you leave, always check the trail conditions and weather reports. Many trails may still be covered in snow or ice in the winter and early spring, so bring crampons or spikes as needed. Furthermore, if you're hiking near rivers, be aware of strong currents and exercise caution when crossing streams.

Tread lightly: Alaska's wilderness areas are fragile and require your protection. To avoid causing plant damage, stick to marked trails whenever possible. Avoid disturbing animals and pack out all trash—leaving no trace is a principle that must be followed when hiking in Alaska.

Chapter 3

Best Hiking Trails in Alaska

3.1. Denali National Park

Denali National Park, home to North America's tallest peak, is one of Alaska's most well-known hiking destinations. The park's rugged landscapes, dense forests, vast tundra, and towering mountain ranges make it an ideal hiking destination. Whether you're looking for a challenging multi-day trek or a short, scenic loop, Denali has a variety of trails that allow hikers to experience Alaska's wild beauty up close. Three of the park's most popular trails are listed below, each with unique views and challenges for hikers of varying skill levels.

1. Denali Summit Trail

The Denali Summit Trail attracts experienced hikers looking for a challenge to test their skills and endurance. However, it is important to note that this is not your typical hike, as summiting Denali (formerly known as Mount McKinley) is a technical climb that requires mountaineering experience and the right equipment. Because of the difficulty and dangers involved, most visitors are unable to reach the summit. But don't let this put you off—the views and adventure surrounding the trail still provide an unforgettable experience for those who are prepared.

The trail starts at the park's base camp and requires extensive preparation, including a multi-week expedition that leads climbers through icy slopes, crevasses, and rocky ridges. It's a physically demanding journey, so hikers should be prepared to face harsh weather, extreme temperatures, and altitude changes as they climb the mountain. If you plan to attempt the summit, make sure you have the necessary equipment, such as crampons, ice axes, and ropes, and consider hiring an experienced guide.

For those who do not wish to summit, there are several excellent viewpoints along the lower sections of the trail from which to appreciate Denali's scale and beauty. Though not for the faint of heart, the Denali Summit Trail provides an unparalleled Alaskan experience for those who have the skills and determination to climb one of the world's highest mountains.

2. Savage River Loop.

The Savage River Loop is an excellent choice for those looking for a shorter, easier hike while still providing breathtaking views of the surrounding Denali landscape. This relatively flat trail, which is about 2 miles long, is appropriate for hikers of all skill levels, including families with children and those who are not physically prepared for a more strenuous hike. It's also an excellent introduction to Denali's natural beauty, with breathtaking views of the Savage River, surrounding valleys, and distant peaks.

The loop begins near the Savage River Campground, crossing the river and winding through a valley surrounded by impressive mountain ranges and rugged terrain. The trail provides excellent opportunities to observe wildlife, such as caribou, moose, and a variety of birds. Along the way, you'll see beautiful wildflowers in the summer, and the changing fall foliage is a photographer's dream. In the winter, the trail transforms into a snowshoeing path, providing a unique perspective on Denali's stunning winter landscape.

The Savage River Loop is also a great trail for people who want to experience Denali without going too far into the backcountry. The trail is well-kept and easy to navigate, making it ideal for beginners or those with limited time.

3. Mount Healy Overlook.

For hikers looking for panoramic views of Denali National Park's wilderness, the Mount Healy Overlook Trail is a must-see. This moderate, 5.4-mile round-trip trail leads you through diverse terrain and to one of the park's most spectacular viewpoints. Although the trail is short, it ascends more than 1,700 feet, making it a moderately challenging hike with breathtaking views as you make your way to the top.

The trailhead is near the Denali Visitor Center, and you'll begin your journey through spruce forests and alpine meadows. As you ascend the trail, the dense forest gives way to more open areas, providing a better view of the surrounding mountains, valleys, and rivers. At the trail's summit, you're rewarded with panoramic views of Denali, the Alaska Range, and the vast landscape below. On a clear day, you can see the entire Denali massif in all its glory, with snow-capped peaks piercing the sky.

The steep hike to Mount Healy Overlook is well worth it for the breathtaking views at the summit. For those who are physically fit and want to challenge themselves without committing to a full-day hike, the Mount Healy Overlook Trail provides the ideal combination of elevation gain, varied scenery, and a memorable experience. It's especially popular with photographers and those who want to capture Denali's grandeur in all its glory.

3.2. Kenai Peninsula

The Kenai Peninsula is one of Alaska's most popular hiking destinations, with a diverse range of trails that lead through lush forests, along rugged coastlines, and to towering glaciers. Whether you're a beginner looking for an easy hike or a seasoned adventurer looking for something more challenging, the Kenai Peninsula has a trail for you. The following are three of the peninsula's most popular and scenic hikes, each highlighting a different aspect of this breathtaking region.

1. Exit Glacier Trail.

The Exit Glacier Trail is one of Alaska's easiest and most accessible trails, making it ideal for those who want to experience the majestic beauty of a glacier without requiring extensive hiking or technical skills. This short, 1-mile round-trip trail in Kenai Fjords National Park provides breathtaking views of Exit Glacier, a dynamic and ever-changing ice mass flowing down from the Harding Icefield.

The trail starts at the Exit Glacier parking lot and winds through a spruce forest before arriving at a viewpoint that provides a close-up view of the glacier. The path is well-kept and simple to navigate, making it ideal for families and casual hikers. Along the way, you'll see signs explaining the glacier's history and movement, as well as the flora and fauna that inhabit the area. During the summer months, the trail offers excellent opportunities for wildflower viewing.

Those looking to extend their visit can hike up to the Glacier Overlook, a more strenuous 3-mile round-trip hike that provides even more dramatic views of Exit Glacier and the surrounding landscape. While the Exit Glacier Trail is not physically demanding, it does provide a unique opportunity to see one of Alaska's most impressive glaciers up close, making it a must-see destination for visitors to the Kenai Peninsula.

2. Resurrection Pass Trail.
The Resurrection Pass Trail is a longer, more difficult hike through the rugged backcountry of the Kenai Peninsula. This trail, which stretches 39 miles from the Seward Highway near Cooper Landing to the town of Hope, provides hikers with a more intimate experience of Alaska's wilderness. It's an excellent choice for those seeking a multi-day adventure that includes stunning scenery, diverse ecosystems, and a sense of solitude.

The trail follows a historic gold rush route and passes through a variety of terrain, including lush forests and alpine meadows. Along the way, you'll cross several rivers, pass through dense forests, and see the Kenai Mountains and Cook Inlet. The trail is relatively remote, making it ideal for those seeking a quiet backcountry experience.

Hikers can choose to complete the entire 39-mile trail or take shorter day hikes. The Resurrection Pass Trail is usually completed in two to four days, with several campsites along the way. These campsites provide scenic views, and many have fire rings and outhouses. If you're planning a longer hike, be prepared for changing weather conditions, as the trail may be muddy or snow-covered, depending on the time of year.

3. Harding Ice Field Trail

For those looking for an unforgettable Alaskan hiking experience, the Harding Icefield Trail is a must-do. This 8.2-mile one-way trail is one of the most popular in Kenai Fjords National Park, with spectacular views of glaciers, snow-capped peaks, and the vast Harding Icefield. The trail is a difficult hike that gains over 3,000 feet in elevation, making it ideal for experienced hikers seeking a strenuous day trek.

The trail begins at the Exit Glacier parking lot and winds through the lush forest before gradually ascending into the alpine zone. As you ascend, the views of Exit Glacier become more dramatic, and by the Harding Icefield Overlook, you'll be treated to an awe-inspiring panoramic view of the icefield, which spans over 700 square miles.

The icefield is a vast expanse of ice and snow with numerous glaciers flowing down into the valleys below.

Hikers should be prepared to face steep, rocky terrain and unpredictable weather conditions. The trail can be especially difficult in the early summer or late fall, when snow and ice may still cover the path. Good footwear, plenty of water, and proper layering are required for this hike. While the ascent is difficult, the reward at the top is well worth it, with breathtaking views of the icefield and surrounding peaks.

The Harding Icefield Trail allows you to extend your hike onto the icefield itself. However, this requires additional equipment, such as crampons, and should only be attempted by those with glacier travel experience or accompanied by a guide.

3.3. Chugach State Park

Chugach State Park, one of the largest state parks in the United States, is located just outside of Anchorage and provides breathtaking views of the Chugach Mountains and surrounding wilderness. The park's diverse trails range from easy walks to more difficult climbs, making it an ideal destination for hikers of all abilities.

The following are two standout trails in Chugach State Park that provide some of the best hiking opportunities in the area.

1. *Flattop Mountain Trail.*

Flattop Mountain is one of the most popular hikes in Chugach State Park, and with good reason. This moderately difficult trail is about 3.3 miles one way and provides some of the best panoramic views of Anchorage, the surrounding mountain ranges, and Cook Inlet. Flattop is a relatively short hike, but it gains significant elevation (about 1,300 feet), making it an excellent choice for those looking to get a good workout while admiring the scenery.

The trailhead is located just off Glen Alps Road, and the path winds through forested areas before transitioning to rocky terrain as you approach the summit. The final section of the trail is steep and can be rocky, so wear sturdy shoes. Hikers who reach the summit are rewarded with breathtaking 360-degree views of Anchorage, the inlet, and distant peaks. On clear days, you can see Alaska's highest peak, Denali, in the distance.

Flattop Mountain is also an excellent location for wildlife watching. Hikers should always be prepared for encounters with wildlife, as moose, mountain goats, and even black bears are common sightings. The trail is open all year, and in the winter, it becomes a popular spot for snowshoeing and winter hiking.

2. Kincaid Park Trails.

Kincaid Park is a popular urban park on Anchorage's western edge. The park's extensive trail network has something for everyone, ranging from easy walks to more difficult treks. Kincaid Park has more than 12 miles of trails, the majority of which are well-maintained and accessible year-round. The park is popular among locals seeking to escape to nature without leaving the city.

Kincaid Park's trails feature a variety of landscapes, including forested areas, coastal bluffs, and panoramic views of the Anchorage skyline. The Kincaid Park Loop is a relatively easy 2.5-mile trail that showcases the park's beauty, including coastal views and wildlife sightings. For those seeking a longer adventure, the park has several interconnected trails that lead into the nearby coastal wetlands and along the shores of Knik Arm.

Kincaid Park is particularly well-known for its wildlife, including moose, bears, and a variety of bird species. In the winter, the park is ideal for cross-country skiing, with groomed trails suitable for both beginners and experienced skiers. Kincaid Park provides a convenient and beautiful hiking experience year-round, right on Anchorage's doorstep.

Wrangell-St. Elias National Park is Alaska's largest national park, with some of the state's most rugged and remote hiking trails. The park is renowned for its glaciers, towering mountains, and pristine wilderness. Hikers can expect to encounter a variety of terrains, from alpine meadows to glaciers, for an experience unlike any other. The following are two popular hiking trails that will lead you through the heart of this magnificent national park.

1. Root Glacier Trail.

The Root Glacier Trail is one of the most accessible and picturesque hikes in Wrangell-St. Elias National Park. This 4.5-mile round-trip trail is suitable for hikers of all skill levels and offers an excellent opportunity to get up close to a glacier. The trail begins at the Kennicott Mine, an abandoned copper mine that adds historical context to the hike. As you hike, you'll see remnants of the mining operation before entering the wilderness, surrounded by the Root Glacier's towering peaks and ice formations.

Along the way, you'll see waterfalls, alpine meadows, and glaciers, and at the end of the trail, you'll have the opportunity to explore the Root Glacier. The glacier is a spectacular sight, and many hikers choose to extend their visit by participating in a guided glacier walk or ice hike, which involves strapping on crampons and walking directly on the glacier surface. For those looking to go even further, the Root Glacier Trail leads to the nearby Donoho Basin, which has more difficult terrain and breathtaking views.

2. Skolai Pass Trail.

The Skolai Pass Trail is a multi-day trek ideal for experienced hikers looking for an authentic Alaskan adventure. This 22-mile one-way trail connects the McCarthy and Nabesna roads in the Wrangell Mountains and is widely regarded as one of Alaska's most scenic and remote trails. The trail winds through wild and rugged terrain, including dense forests, alpine tundra, and pristine rivers, offering views of the surrounding glaciers and mountain peaks.

The Skolai Pass Trail is difficult due to its length and varied terrain, but it provides a unique opportunity to experience the untouched wilderness of Wrangell-St. Elias National Park. Hikers should be prepared for stream crossings, elevation changes, and possibly harsh weather conditions, as this is a backcountry trail with limited amenities. The reward, however, is a sense of solitude and the chance to see some of the world's most beautiful natural landscapes.

In addition to its breathtaking scenery, Skolai Pass is a popular route for nature lovers. Bears, moose, caribou, and a variety of bird species can be seen throughout the park, so keep an eye out while hiking. Skolai Pass offers a true wilderness experience that is ideal for those looking for a challenging and rewarding adventure in the heart of Alaska.

3.5 Glacier Bay National Park.

Glacier Bay National Park in southeastern Alaska is known for its breathtaking scenery, which includes towering glaciers, mist-covered mountains, and a diverse marine life. The park has several hiking trails that allow visitors to explore its rugged landscapes while taking in breathtaking views of glaciers and pristine wilderness. The following are two notable trails in Glacier Bay National Park that offer a glimpse into the area's natural beauty and wildlife.

1. Bartlett Cove Trail.

The Bartlett Cove Trail is one of the easiest and most accessible hikes in Glacier Bay National Park. This relatively short 1.5-mile loop trail is located near the park's visitor center in Bartlett Cove, making it ideal for those looking to explore the area without embarking on a strenuous hike. The trail winds through a temperate rainforest, providing an excellent introduction to the park's diverse ecosystems.

The trail will take you through lush forests teeming with towering Sitka spruce and hemlock trees, ferns, and mosses. The trail also passes through tidal flats, where you may see seabirds, otters, seals, and even whales in the bay. The trail provides views of nearby Bartlett Cove and is an excellent spot for bird watching, particularly in the early morning or evening when wildlife is most active.

Although the Bartlett Cove Trail is short, it offers an excellent opportunity to learn about the region's ecology and history. Along the way, interpretive signs provide information on the local flora and fauna, the area's indigenous history, and the cove's significance in Alaska's maritime heritage.

This trail is ideal for families, first-time hikers, or anyone looking for a relaxing stroll through one of Alaska's most scenic coastal environments. It's also an excellent place to start your exploration of Glacier Bay National Park before progressing to more difficult trails.

2. Mount Fairweather Trail.

For experienced hikers looking for a more challenging and rewarding hike, the Mount Fairweather Trail provides an unforgettable opportunity. This trail is a strenuous multi-day trek that covers approximately 11 miles one way and leads to the base of Mount Fairweather, one of the region's highest mountains. The trail provides some of the most breathtaking views of Glacier Bay National Park, including sweeping vistas of glaciers, mountains, and the surrounding wilderness.

The Mount Fairweather Trail begins at the end of the Bartlett Cove road system, but unlike the Bartlett Cove Trail, it requires careful planning due to its length, elevation gain, and remote location. The hike takes you through temperate rainforests, wildflower-filled meadows, and alpine environments. Hikers will encounter rugged terrain, creeks, and glacial runoff along the way, making the trail difficult to navigate during the spring and early summer months when the snow melts.

Mount Fairweather's summit, while difficult to reach, offers stunning panoramic views of Glacier Bay, including close-up views of glaciers calving into the bay below. At higher elevations, you can observe the area's diverse flora and fauna, which includes mountain goats, marmots, and a variety of bird species.

Due to the trail's difficulty and remoteness, hikers must be well prepared. This includes bringing appropriate hiking gear for rugged terrain, staying aware of weather conditions, and having navigation tools like a map, compass, or GPS. Furthermore, bear safety precautions should be taken because the trail runs through areas where bears are known to roam.

While difficult, the Mount Fairweather Trail provides an unparalleled hiking experience for those who are prepared and want to see the grandeur of Glacier Bay's wilderness from a breathtaking vantage point.

Southeast Alaska is a region of rugged beauty with temperate rainforests, majestic glaciers, and towering mountains. The region provides some of the best hiking opportunities in the state, with trails winding through lush forests, scenic coastlines, and up to panoramic vistas. The three standout hiking trails in Southeast Alaska listed below allow visitors to fully explore this stunning area.

1. Mendenhall Glacier Trail.

The Mendenhall Glacier Trail is one of Southeast Alaska's most popular and accessible hikes. Located just outside of Juneau, the trail provides a breathtaking view of the 12-mile-long Mendenhall Glacier, one of the region's most famous glaciers. This 1.5-mile loop trail is relatively easy, making it suitable for hikers of all skill levels, and it offers one of the best opportunities to see the glacier up close.

The trail begins at the Mendenhall Glacier Visitor Center and leads through lush spruce, hemlock, and alder forests, with glimpses of the glacier's ice-blue face visible through the trees. The trail gradually leads to a viewing platform from which hikers can observe the glacier and the surrounding landscape. The Mendenhall Glacier itself is breathtaking, with its massive ice flow feeding into the Mendenhall River, which frequently has icebergs floating in its waters.

For those looking to broaden their experience, the Mendenhall Glacier also provides opportunities for kayaking and ice hiking on the glacier. The area is abundant with wildlife, including black bears, bald eagles, and a variety of other bird species. The Mendenhall Glacier Trail is especially beautiful in the early morning or late evening, when the light softens and the area becomes quieter, allowing you to fully appreciate the landscape's serene beauty.

2. Mount Juneau Trail.

Mount Juneau provides an exhilarating and more difficult hike for experienced hikers seeking to summit one of Juneau's most iconic peaks. This 3.5-mile trail is steep and strenuous, with an elevation gain of approximately 3,000 feet, but the views at the top are well worth it.

The trail begins near the end of Basin Road and climbs steadily through dense forest, rocky outcrops, and alpine meadows. As you ascend, the views open up, revealing increasingly spectacular views of downtown Juneau, the surrounding islands, and the surrounding coastline. Hikers who reach the summit are rewarded with a breathtaking panoramic view that extends to the waters of the Gastineau Channel and the surrounding mountains.

Along the way, you'll pass through a variety of ecosystems, including temperate rainforests and alpine tundra. It's an excellent hike for those looking to experience the stark contrast between the lower forested areas and the upper alpine environment. The trail is well-maintained, but it can be steep and rocky in places, so wear sturdy shoes. Hikers should expect a strenuous ascent due to its steepness, but the sense of accomplishment and sweeping views from the top make this a memorable trek.

If you're looking for a difficult hike with a big payoff, the Mount Juneau Trail is a must-see in Southeast Alaska.

3. Tongass National Forest Trails.

The Tongass National Forest, the largest national forest in the United States, covers more than 16 million acres and has a vast network of hiking trails that span a wide range of ecosystems, from coastal rainforests to alpine ridgelines. The forest is home to a diverse range of wildlife, including bears, wolves, and hundreds of bird species, making it an ideal destination for nature and wildlife enthusiasts.

The Tongass National Forest offers numerous hiking opportunities, but one of the most popular and scenic trails is the Hiker's Cove Trail, which is located near the town of Sitka. This 2.5-mile trail leads you through old-growth forests and along the coast, with stunning views of the surrounding waters and islands. The trail is relatively easy, making it ideal for families or new hikers.

For those looking for more difficult hikes, the Baranof Falls Trail is a rugged 6-mile round-trip trek through a lush rainforest. Hikers pass several waterfalls and enjoy breathtaking views of the surrounding mountains and coastal wilderness.

The sense of remoteness and isolation provided by the Tongass National Forest's trails is one of its most distinguishing features. While many of the trails are well-marked and accessible, hikers may find themselves deep in the forest, surrounded by towering trees and wildlife, with few signs of human activity. It's a place where hikers can fully appreciate Southeast Alaska's wild beauty.

The Tongass National Forest is also an excellent choice for those looking to combine hiking with other outdoor activities like kayaking, fishing, and wildlife viewing. There are numerous remote cabins and campsites scattered throughout the forest, allowing hikers to spend multiple days in the wilderness and fully immerse themselves in the area's natural beauty.

Chapter 4

Useful Info for Hikers

4.1. How to Go to Alaska

Alaska, known for its remote and untamed wilderness, is more accessible than it appears. Whether you're flying in from another state, driving up the Alaska Highway, or taking a ferry to the state's coastal towns, getting to Alaska takes some planning. Here's a breakdown of the main modes of transportation for getting to the Last Frontier, as well as the best ways to get around the state once you arrive.

1. Airports, Highways, and Transportation Options.
AirportsThe most common way to travel to Alaska is by air, and the state has several major airports, the largest of which is in Anchorage. Flying is the most efficient and time-saving option, particularly if you're coming from outside Alaska.

Ted Stevens Anchorage International Airport(ANC):
Located in Anchorage, this is the state's busiest airport and serves as the primary hub for most domestic and international flights. Anchorage is a popular starting point for visitors wanting to explore both the interior and southern Alaska. From here, you can easily travel to other parts of the state via smaller airports.

Fairbanks International Airport (FAI) is a major airport in the heart of Alaska that serves those looking to explore the state's interior or the Arctic regions. It offers flights to Anchorage and other Alaskan cities, as well as direct flights to the lower 48 states.

Juneau International Airport (JNU): As the state capital, Juneau is a popular starting point for visitors to Southeast Alaska, particularly Glacier Bay and the Tongass National Forest. Juneau is not accessible by road, but it has regular flights from Anchorage, Seattle, and other major cities.

Ketchikan International Airport (KTN): Serving Alaska's southernmost town, Ketchikan is an important gateway to the state's southeastern region. Ketchikan is a popular stop for cruise ships, with direct flights from Seattle and other regional airports.

Other airports include Sitka (SIT), Seward (SWD), and Wrangell (WRG), which are more remote but well-connected for those interested in exploring smaller towns or coastal regions. Many of these airports offer daily commuter flights or seasonal flights, particularly during the peak tourist season in the summer.

Highways and Driving to Alaska.

Driving to Alaska is a must-do for the adventurous traveler who enjoys scenic road trips. The most popular route is the Alaska Highway, which starts in Dawson Creek, British Columbia and runs 1,390 miles through the Yukon Territory and eventually into Alaska. Travelers can take this road from the continental United States and enter Alaska via the Tok Cutoff, which leads to Tok, Alaska, where they can connect to other parts of the state.

The Alaska Highway is an epic road trip that offers breathtaking views of forests, lakes, and mountainous landscapes. Though the highway is well-maintained, it is critical to plan for long distances between services such as gas stations and restaurants, particularly in more remote areas. Driving this route typically takes 2 to 3 days, depending on your starting point and pace.

The Richardson Highway and Glenn Highway also connect major towns in Alaska, such as Fairbanks and Anchorage. From Anchorage, visitors can travel by road to the Kenai Peninsula or the breathtaking Denali National Park.

While driving is a popular way to explore Alaska's main roads, it's important to remember that many parts of the state are inaccessible by car, especially in the more remote wilderness areas. Valdez, Denali, and Seward are all accessible by car, but other hiking destinations, such as Wrangell-St. Elias National Park or Gates of the Arctic may require the use of small planes or boats.

Ferries

Alaska's coastal areas, such as Southeast Alaska and the Panhandle, are best accessed by ferry. The Alaska Marine Highway System operates a network of ferries that connects major coastal towns from Bellingham, Washington, through the Inside Passage, and to the Aleutian Islands.

The ferry system is especially useful if you're coming from the Lower 48 or Canada and want to visit places like Ketchikan, Juneau, and Sitka. These ferries carry passengers and, in some cases, vehicles. The ferry ride itself is an experience, with stunning views of fjords, glaciers, and marine life along the way.

Ferries also serve an important role in connecting communities in Alaska, making them one of the most efficient ways to visit the state's more remote coastal towns. However, ferry routes are seasonal, with the majority of routes operating during the summer months when the weather is more pleasant.

Transportation Within Alaska

Once you arrive in Alaska, your transportation options vary depending on the region you're exploring. Here's a guide to getting around:

Renting A Car: In larger cities such as Anchorage and Fairbanks, renting a car is a convenient and practical way to get around. It allows you to explore the surrounding areas at your own pace, including Denali National Park, the Kenai Peninsula, and the Wrangell-St. Elias region. However, rental car availability in remote areas may be limited.

Small Aircraft: Many of Alaska's remote areas, such as national parks and wilderness areas, are best reached by small aircraft. Many charter companies in Alaska offer flights to areas that are inaccessible by road. For example, to fully experience Wrangell-St. Elias National Park and Gates of the Arctic, air travel is required. Remember to book these flights in advance, especially during peak hiking seasons.

Shuttle Services and Tours: If you don't want to drive or navigate public transportation, Alaska offers a variety of shuttle services and guided tours. These services can transport you to popular destinations such as Denali National Park, the Kenai Peninsula, and even specific trailheads in Glacier Bay.

Public Transportation: Public bus systems in Alaska's larger cities (Anchorage, Fairbanks, and Juneau) provide routes that allow you to travel within the city limits. However, once you leave urban areas, public transportation options become limited, so if you're traveling to remote areas, you should plan for rental cars or guided tours.

4.2. Transportation in Alaska

Once you've arrived in Alaska, navigating the vast state to reach your hiking destinations and explore its many wilderness areas will require some planning. Because of Alaska's size and remoteness, transportation options vary greatly depending on your destination. There are numerous options for getting around this beautiful state, including renting a car, taking a shuttle, or taking a boat ride.

1. Shuttle Services, Rental Cars, and Boat Rides
Shuttle Services

Shuttle services are an excellent way to travel around Alaska, especially in areas with numerous hiking opportunities. Many towns and popular hiking destinations have shuttle services that provide easy access to trailheads, lodging, and local attractions. For example, during the summer months, shuttle buses transport visitors to various trailheads, campgrounds, and other park locations. These shuttles are an excellent choice if you're visiting areas where parking is limited or want to avoid the hassle of driving on winding, sometimes unpaved roads.

In addition to park shuttles, towns such as Anchorage, Seward, and Fairbanks offer shuttle services to help visitors get around. Many of these services provide transportation to popular hiking areas or cruise ship terminals for those planning to explore Alaska's coastal regions. These shuttles are frequently used by hikers who do not want to rent a car but need to get to trailheads or other important locations.

Rental vehicles

Renting a car in Alaska is a popular and flexible way to explore the state. Renting a car or RV allows you to travel at your own pace and get off the beaten path, whether you're visiting Denali National Park or the Kenai Peninsula or exploring coastal towns. Major cities such as Anchorage and Fairbanks have several rental agencies that offer a diverse range of vehicles, from compact cars to SUVs and 4x4s, which are especially useful on Alaska's more rugged roads.

While rental cars are widely available, it's important to remember that some areas, such as remote national parks and wild wilderness areas, can only be reached by air or boat, so plan accordingly if you're venturing far from major roads. During the summer, many rental companies will provide vehicles suitable for Alaska's varied terrain, including all-wheel drive vehicles for those traveling to more remote areas.

If you're traveling in the winter, you should rent a vehicle with snow tires and be prepared for icy roads and winter weather conditions. Popular routes such as the Alaska Highway and Richardson Highway can be difficult to navigate in the winter, so check road conditions before heading out.

Boat Rides

Boat rides are an essential mode of transportation for those seeking to explore Alaska's coastal regions and remote wilderness. The Alaska Marine Highway System, a network of ferries, is one of the most convenient ways to reach coastal towns, islands, and national parks. The ferry system runs routes from Bellingham, Washington, to Southeast Alaska, making stops in Juneau, Ketchikan, Sitka, and Skagway. Traveling by ferry allows you to explore Alaska's Inside Passage, which is one of the world's most scenic and pristine waterways.

In addition to the Alaska Marine Highway, smaller private boat services are commonly used to reach remote coastal communities and national parks such as Glacier Bay National Park and Wrangell-St. Elias National Park. Many fishing lodges, wildlife tour companies, and hiking groups use boats to take guests to trailheads or backcountry campsites along the coast. If you're planning a hiking trip that includes visits to remote islands or areas like the Tongass National Forest, boat rides may be your only option for getting there.

Additionally, Alaska Wilderness Adventures and Guided Fishing Trips frequently combine boat rides with hiking, transporting visitors through fjords, along glaciers, and across tranquil rivers to hiking destinations that would otherwise be inaccessible by land.

4.3. Important Travel Information.

When planning your hiking trip in Alaska, you should know where to stay and how to get to essential services and amenities. Alaska's vast wilderness and remote locations provide a unique experience for outdoor enthusiasts, but they also pose challenges in terms of accommodations, supplies, and support. Here's a guide to help you plan your trip, including all of the information you'll need to stay comfortable, safe, and prepared.

1. Where to Stay

Alaska has a diverse range of accommodations, from basic campgrounds and backcountry huts to luxurious lodges and charming bed-and-breakfasts. Where you choose to stay is largely determined by the type of experience you seek, your budget, and the area you intend to explore. The following are the main types of accommodations you'll find throughout the state:

Hotels and lodges: Anchorage, Fairbanks, Juneau, and Ketchikan have a wide range of hotels, motels, and lodges to suit both budget-conscious and upscale travelers. Some of these places have hot tubs, saunas, and even spas, making them ideal for relaxing after a long day of hiking.

Denali National Park also has several lodges nearby, providing easy access to the park's entrance and popular hiking trails, such as the Savage River Loop.

Backcountry Cabins and Huts: For those seeking adventure, Alaska's backcountry offers rustic cabins and huts for rent. These cabins are typically found in remote areas and provide basic shelter for hikers visiting national parks such as Denali and Wrangell-St. Elias. Booking these cabins in advance is strongly advised, especially during the busy summer months. Many of these accommodations are located along popular trails, making them a convenient option for those who want to camp but prefer to sleep under a roof at night.

Campgrounds: Alaska has numerous public and private campgrounds, many of which are near trailheads and national parks. Denali National Park, for example, has several campgrounds, including Riley Creek Campground, which is open during the summer season. Most campgrounds provide basic amenities such as picnic tables, fire pits, and restrooms; however, it is important to note that campsites can fill up quickly, particularly during peak season. Reservations for campgrounds on the Kenai Peninsula and Southeast Alaska should be made well in advance.

Glamping and One-of-a-Kind Stays: Alaska offers *glamping* or glamorous camping experiences for those who want to enjoy nature without having to rough it.

These upscale tents or yurts have comfortable beds, often with stunning views, and may include additional amenities such as a private bathroom or gourmet meals. These accommodations are available near popular parks such as the Kenai Peninsula and Wrangell-St. Elias National Park provides an alternative to traditional camping.

Airbnb and Vacation Rentals: Visitors to larger towns and cities can enjoy a home-away-from-home experience through Airbnb and vacation rentals. Renting a cabin or house is a great option if you're traveling with a group or family and need more space and privacy. Many of these homes are located in scenic areas, so you can wake up to mountain views or nearby forests.

When planning your trip to Alaska, make sure to look for amenities like Wi-Fi, heating, and food options, particularly in more remote areas. The weather in the state can be unpredictable, so having a comfortable place to retreat to after a long day of hiking is critical to your well-being.

2. Finding Services and Amenities.
While Alaska's rugged beauty provides many advantages for outdoor adventures, it's critical to plan for the services and amenities you'll require along the way. Access to supplies, food, and medical services can be limited in remote areas, so knowing what is available in different regions will help you plan a successful trip.

Grocery stores and food supply: Larger cities such as Anchorage, Fairbanks, and Juneau have numerous grocery stores where you can stock up on food for your hikes, including both chain supermarkets and local shops. The main grocery store chains in the state are Safeway, Fred Meyer, and Costco, which sell a wide variety of fresh produce, snacks, and camping supplies. Look for specialized outdoor gear or fresh produce at local markets or specialty stores.

Grocery stores in more remote areas, such as Wrangell-St. Elias or Gates of the Arctic National Park can be scarce and carry only a limited selection of items. If you're hiking in these areas, make sure to plan your meals and bring everything you'll need. Many towns along the Alaska Marine Highway or near trailheads will have small general stores where you can purchase necessities such as canned goods, stove fuel, and first aid supplies.

Fuel and gasoline stations: Fuel stations in Alaska can be scarce, particularly in more remote areas. If you're driving to your hiking destinations, make sure to fill up your gas tank before entering the wilderness, especially if you intend to travel along the Alaska Highway or to areas like Wrangell-St. Elias, where fuel may be scarce. Be aware that fuel prices in Alaska may be higher than in the Lower 48, particularly in more remote areas. If you're driving to more remote locations, bring extra fuel.

Medical Services and Emergency Assistance: Because Alaska is remote, emergency medical services may be limited in some areas, so you should be aware of the locations of hospitals or urgent care centers along your route. Anchorage and Fairbanks have well-equipped medical facilities, but in small towns, particularly in the Alaska Panhandle or Wrangell-St. Elias, medical care may be limited to clinics. If you're heading into more remote wilderness, bring a first aid kit and be prepared for basic medical emergencies. Furthermore, many trailheads and remote locations may be covered by emergency helicopter services, which can provide evacuation in the event of an injury, though at a high cost.

Wi-Fi, Cell Service, and Communication: Cell phone service can be spotty in Alaska's remote regions, particularly in the backcountry. In more developed areas such as Anchorage, Fairbanks, and Juneau, Wi-Fi is available in hotels, cafes, and public areas. However, once you're out in the wilderness, internet access and phone signals may become unreliable. If you're planning a long-distance hike in a remote area, rent a satellite phone or bring a personal locator beacon (PLB) for emergency communication. Many tour companies also provide satellite communication devices to their guests in the event of an emergency.

4.4. Food and Dining for Hikers.

When embarking on a hiking adventure in Alaska, you must plan ahead of time for both trail food and off-trail meals. Whether you're trekking through Denali's rugged landscapes or exploring the coastal beauty of the Kenai Peninsula, having the right food can help you stay energized while admiring the breathtaking views. Alaska's food culture is as diverse as its wilderness, with an emphasis on fresh, locally sourced ingredients. Whether you bring your trail snacks or plan to dine in the various towns and cities, you'll have plenty of options to keep you satisfied.

1. Packing Trail Snacks.

One of the most important aspects of preparing for an Alaskan hike is bringing the right snacks. Because Alaska's trails can be remote and long, you'll want to bring lightweight, high-energy food to keep you going. Hiking often involves long stretches between designated stopping points, so having snacks that are both nutritious and portable is essential.

Energy bars are one of the simplest and most convenient high-energy snacks to prepare. These bars are designed to provide a well-balanced mix of protein, carbohydrates, and healthy fats, all of which are necessary for energy maintenance. Popular brands include Clif Bar, Kind Bars, and RXBAR. Another great option is trail mix, which can be made with a variety of nuts, dried fruits, and even chocolate or candy for a sweet treat. Nuts like almonds or cashews are high in healthy fats and protein, whereas dried fruits like raisins or apricots are high in natural sugars, providing a quick energy boost.

Beef jerky is an excellent source of protein and is especially popular for longer hikes due to its shelf stability. It's a light snack that doesn't need refrigeration, making it ideal for hiking through Alaska's wilderness. If you want something more substantial, try instant oatmeal packets, which you can easily prepare by adding hot water during a rest stop. These provide a warm, satisfying meal to get you through the colder mornings and evenings on the trail.

Additionally, you should pack plenty of water or a hydration system, as staying hydrated in Alaska's sometimes extreme weather conditions is critical. Some hikers prefer to use hydration packs (such as CamelBak) for quick access to water while keeping their hands free. If you prefer bottles, make sure you have enough to get through long stretches, especially on trails where water sources are scarce.

2. Recommended Restaurants and Cafés
After a long day of hiking, the last thing you want to think about is where you're going to eat next. Alaska's towns and cities are home to a diverse range of local restaurants that highlight the region's distinct flavors, particularly its plentiful seafood and wild game. Whether

you're in the heart of Anchorage or a small coastal town like Seward, you'll have plenty of dining options.

Anchorage offers a variety of restaurants that reflect the region's diverse influences. For a traditional local experience, visit Marx Bros Café, which is known for its elegant decor and menu of fresh seafood and prime cuts of meat. If you're looking for something more casual, Moose's Tooth Pub & Pizzeria is a local favorite that serves hearty pizzas alongside a selection of craft beers. For a more refined meal, Simon & Seafort's Saloon & Grill offers sweeping views of Cook Inlet and a seafood-heavy menu featuring king crab and halibut.

If you're in Seward, known for its proximity to Kenai Fjords National Park, try Resurrection Roadhouse, which specializes in local fish and meats, or The Cookery, which serves dishes made with ingredients sourced from the surrounding area. Both locations provide an excellent post-hike meal to replenish after a long day on the trails. Don't miss Chinooks Waterfront Restaurant, a local favorite with delicious seafood and spectacular harbor views.

Fairbanks' restaurant scene reflects the city's laid-back atmosphere. The Cookie Jar Restaurant serves hearty breakfasts and freshly baked goods, making it an ideal place to refuel before a hike. If you're looking for local Alaskan cuisine, The Pump House serves specialties like caribou and wild salmon in a cozy and historic setting.

Spenard Builders Supply is a good place to get a casual meal with locally brewed beers and comfort foods.

3. Specialties of Alaskan Local Cuisine

Alaska's cuisine reflects the state's natural bounty, featuring fresh fish, wild game, and locally grown produce. Because of the state's long history of fishing and hunting, the local food scene focuses on a connection to the land and waters. If you want to try Alaskan cuisine during your trip, here are a few recommendations.

Salmon is perhaps Alaska's most recognizable dish. It appears on menus throughout the state, whether grilled, smoked, or served in more traditional preparations such as salmon chowder or salmon roe. Alaska's wild-caught king salmon is highly prized for its rich flavor and tender texture, and it is frequently served as a fillet or even sushi. Halibut is another popular option for those who prefer a richer fish, which can be prepared in a variety of ways, such as battered and fried, grilled, or in fish tacos.

For a truly Alaskan experience, try wild game meats like moose or caribou. These meats can be found in a variety of dishes, including steaks and hamburgers, as well as hearty stews and casseroles. These game meats have a robust flavor that complements the earthy herbs and spices common in Alaskan cuisine.

No trip to Alaska is complete without trying king crab, which is served in a variety of ways, most notably steamed and served with melted butter. The crab meat's sweet, delicate flavor is a true delicacy, and it is widely regarded as one of the best meals available in the state. Many of Alaska's coastal towns have specialty restaurants that serve freshly caught crab.

For dessert, try *akutaq*, also known as Eskimo ice cream, a traditional dessert made from whipped fat, berries, and sugar. While it may appear unusual, it provides a distinct taste of Alaska's indigenous culinary traditions.

Chapter 5

Accommodation Options in Alaska

When it comes to accommodations in Alaska, there are numerous options available to hikers of all types. Whether you want a cozy cabin in the wilderness, a luxurious resort with breathtaking views, or a rustic backcountry camping experience, Alaska has it all. Accommodation options vary not only in style but also in location, ranging from remote cabins nestled in pristine wilderness to bustling lodges near popular trailheads. Below, we'll look at the best lodging, camping, and unique stays to make your hiking trip more enjoyable.

5.1. Lodging Options

1. Denali Lodging

When planning a trip to Denali National Park, it's critical to select accommodations that provide convenience and comfort after a long day on the trails. Denali has a variety of lodging options, including rustic cabins and luxurious resorts.

Denali Bluffs Hotels: Located just outside the park's entrance, this hotel offers guests stunning views of the surrounding landscape as well as easy access to the park. The rooms are spacious, and many have private balconies where you can observe the local wildlife. It's an excellent base for hikers, with shuttle services that take visitors deeper into the park.

McKinley Chalet Resort: For those looking for a more upscale experience, McKinley Chalet Resort provides a range of accommodations, from quaint cabins to elegant hotel rooms. The resort, located along the Nenana River, also includes a restaurant and full-service amenities, making it an excellent choice for those seeking a little extra luxury after their hikes. It's also in an ideal location for exploring the park.

Kantishna Roadhouse: For a more immersive experience, consider staying at the Kantishna Roadhouse, which is deep within the park. This remote lodge, accessible only by shuttle bus or plane, provides a unique opportunity to explore Denali's backcountry. The lodge offers meals, lodging, and guided tours, making it an ideal place to unwind after an adventurous day in the wilderness.

2. Kenai Peninsula Resorts.

The Kenai Peninsula has a wide range of lodging options, from cozy cabins to upscale resorts, many with breathtaking views of the mountains or the ocean.

The Kenai Peninsula Resort: Located near Kenai, this resort provides guests with comfortable accommodations as well as easy access to the area's hiking trails. Guests can enjoy cabin rentals with stunning views of the nearby mountains and ocean.

Resurrection Bay Campground & Cabins: Located in the scenic town of Seward, this establishment provides cozy cabins that are ideal for those looking to explore Kenai Fjords National Park. With hiking trails nearby, this is an excellent base for adventurers, and its proximity to Resurrection Bay allows guests to enjoy boat rides or wildlife-viewing tours.

Seward Windsong Lodge: This lodge, located along the scenic Resurrection River, offers a variety of accommodations, including cabins and suites. The Seward Windsong Lodge is not only a comfortable place to stay, but it also has easy access to hiking trails, such as the popular Harding Icefield Trail.

3. Chugach State Park Lodges.
Chugach State Park, just outside Anchorage, is one of Alaska's largest and most accessible parks, with breathtaking views and a variety of hiking trails. While there are few lodges in the park itself, there are several excellent options nearby.

Girdwood Hotels: Girdwood Hotel is an excellent choice for those looking to combine the park's hiking trails with a resort-style experience. It is located in the small town of Girdwood, which is known for its scenic beauty and as a hub for outdoor activities. This hotel provides comfortable rooms, a restaurant, and convenient access to nearby hiking trails, including Flattop Mountain.

Alyeska Resort: A luxury resort near the park that offers hiking, skiing, and other outdoor activities. The resort has stunning views of the surrounding mountains and trails suitable for all skill levels. It's the ideal spot to unwind after a long day of hiking in Chugach State Park.

5.2. Camping in Alaska.

For those seeking a more immersive experience, camping in Alaska allows them to connect fully with the wilderness. Outdoor enthusiasts have many options, whether they want to stay in designated campgrounds, explore the backcountry, or go winter camping.

1. Denali campgrounds and national parks.

Denali National Park and other national parks in Alaska provide both front-country and backcountry camping opportunities.

Denali National Park's campgrounds: Denali has a few main campgrounds for visitors, including Riley Creek Campground, which is open all year, and Teklanika Campground, which is accessible by shuttle bus and allows campers to stay for multiple nights. These campgrounds are well-equipped with basic amenities such as restrooms and fire rings, and they serve as excellent starting points for hikes throughout the park.

Kennecott Campground (Wrangell-St. Elias): Wrangell-St. Elias National Park has a few developed campgrounds, including the Kennecott Campground, which offers a mix of tent and RV sites. It's an excellent base for exploring nearby trails such as the Root Glacier Trail and the Skolai Pass Trail.

2. Backcountry camping in Alaska.

Alaska's backcountry provides opportunities for adventurous hikers to camp in some of the world's most remote and pristine wilderness areas. Whether in Denali, Kenai, or Wrangell-St. Elias, these areas allow you to camp away from the crowds and truly experience the wilderness.

Backcountry Permits: To camp in Alaska's backcountry, you typically need a backcountry permit, which protects camping areas and reduces environmental impact. Permits are typically available from the park or trail management authority.

Pack In, Pack Out: Follow the Leave No Trace principles and pack out all of your waste, including toilet paper and food scraps. Some campgrounds also require campers to bring bear-resistant food containers.

3. Tips for Remote and Winter Camping.

➤ Winter camping in Alaska can be a challenging yet rewarding experience. The key to success in these circumstances is preparation.
➤ Cold Weather Gear: Make sure your sleeping bags, clothing, and tents are rated for cold weather.
➤ Know the risks: Understanding the potential dangers of winter camping, such as avalanches or extreme temperatures, is critical for safety.
➤ Plan for limited daylight: In the winter, daylight hours are extremely limited, so plan your hikes and camp setups around available light.

5.3. Unique Stays for Hikers

Alaska has a variety of unique and memorable lodging options that go beyond traditional hotels and campgrounds. These options offer both comfort and an authentic Alaskan experience, deepening your connection to the wilderness.

1. Alaska Wilderness Cabins

Staying in a remote wilderness cabin can be an unforgettable experience for those looking for solitude and immersion in Alaska's wild. Many of these cabins are only accessible by boat, plane, or long hikes, making them ideal for those seeking complete isolation.

Denali Backcountry Lodge: Located in Denali National Park, this lodge offers a luxurious yet rustic cabin experience in the heart of the wilderness. The lodge is only accessible via a 90-minute flight, and its location allows guests to enjoy incredible hiking, wildlife watching, and a true Alaskan escape.

Kachemak Bay Wilderness Lodge: This lodge, accessible only by boat or plane, allows guests to stay in cozy cabins located in a remote area of Kachemak Bay State Park. It's ideal for those looking for a one-of-a-kind wilderness experience as it offers hiking, kayaking, and wildlife-viewing opportunities.

2. Glamping in Yurts

If you prefer a more comfortable camping experience, glamping (glamorous camping) and staying in a yurt are excellent choices. Both offer a unique way to connect with nature while remaining comfortable.

Kachemak Bay Glamping: This glamping site, located near Homer, features beautifully appointed tents with beds, lighting, and even private bathrooms. Guests can enjoy a luxurious yet rustic stay amidst pristine wilderness.

Yurts in Denali: Denali National Park has several yurt-style cabins that are ideal for those looking for a comfortable yet rugged stay. These yurts are outfitted with wood stoves, providing a unique and comfortable experience while remaining close to nature.

3. Hostels & Community Lodges

If you want a more affordable and social experience, Alaska has several hostels and community lodges that cater to hikers. These places frequently provide shared rooms, kitchens, and the chance to meet other travelers.

Hostel Anchorage: The Hostel is located in downtown Anchorage and offers affordable and comfortable accommodations. It's an excellent choice for hikers who want to meet other travelers while remaining close to the city's amenities.

The Talkeetna Hostel: Talkeetna, a small town that serves as the gateway to Denali, has a cozy hostel that provides affordable lodging for hikers and adventurers. It's an excellent base for exploring the area before venturing into the wilderness.

Chapter 6

Cultural and historical insights

Hiking in Alaska is more than just an adventure through breathtaking scenery; it's a journey through history. Indigenous peoples lived on and traveled these lands long before the trails were mapped and marked for modern hikers, guided by a deep understanding of the terrain, wildlife, and seasonal variations. Their traditions, stories, and way of life all reflect their strong connection to the land. Understanding this rich cultural history enriches the hiking experience, making each step an opportunity to appreciate the people who have lived in these landscapes for thousands of years.

6.1. Indigenous Peoples of Alaska

Alaska is home to a diverse group of Indigenous peoples, each with their traditions, languages, and histories shaped by the land they live on. For thousands of years, they have coexisted with the harsh wilderness, surviving and flourishing in some of the most extreme conditions on Earth. Unlike modern visitors who arrive with hiking boots, insulated jackets, and GPS devices, these communities learned to navigate the harsh climate through generations of knowledge—reading the land, the skies, and animal behavior for survival.

Indigenous groups in Alaska have traditionally been classified according to their geographic regions and ways of life. In the far north, the Inupiat and Yupik peoples adapted to the Arctic environment by hunting seals, walruses, and whales. Inland, the Athabascan people thrived in the vast boreal forests, tracking caribou and fishing along the many rivers that run through Alaska's interior. Along the southeastern coast, the Tlingit, Haida, and Tsimshian established complex societies with strong artistic traditions, erecting towering totem poles and elaborate longhouses while subsisting on the Pacific's abundant marine resources. Further south and across the Aleutian Islands, the Aleut and Alutiiq peoples developed a fishing-centric lifestyle, using their extensive knowledge of the ocean and weather to navigate the treacherous waters in handcrafted kayaks.

These groups did more than just survive in Alaska's harsh environment; they thrived, developing rich cultures that celebrated their deep respect for nature. Many of their practices are still in use today, demonstrating the resilience and tenacity of Alaska's indigenous people.

History, Culture, and Traditions of Native Alaskans

Alaska's Indigenous history dates back more than 12,000 years, beginning with early migrations across the Bering Land Bridge, a now-submerged connection that once linked Alaska to Siberia. As these early settlers spread across Alaska's vast landscape, they adapted to its diverse environments, establishing distinct cultural traditions that continue to this day.

Storytelling was an important aspect of these traditions. Without a written language, history and knowledge were transmitted through oral narratives, songs, and dances. These stories discussed creation, ancestral wisdom, and lessons from nature. Many of these stories are still important parts of Native culture, being told in homes, schools, and community gatherings.

Art and craftsmanship flourished in these cultures, demonstrating their deep spiritual connection to the land and its creatures. The Tlingit, Haida, and Tsimshian peoples of the southeast became well-known for their intricate carvings, woven cedar bark garments, and vibrant totem poles, each of which told a unique story about family history, historical events, or spiritual beliefs. In the Arctic, the Inupiat and Yupik created magnificent ivory carvings and masks for ceremonial use, while the Athabascans honed their beadwork skills, creating intricate patterns inspired by the natural surroundings.

Subsistence living—hunting, fishing, and gathering—was and remains the foundation of Indigenous life. While modern conveniences have changed some aspects of daily life, many Native Alaskans continue to hunt in traditional ways, fish in ancestral waters, and harvest plants for medicine and food. Nature, for them, is a living entity that must be respected and protected rather than a resource to be exploited.

Cultural Practices and Traditions
To truly appreciate the cultural heritage of Alaska's Indigenous peoples, one must first understand the traditions that continue to shape their lives.

1. Subsistence living.
Even in the modern era, many Native Alaskan communities practice subsistence hunting and fishing. Caribou, moose, salmon, and berries provide sustenance during the long winters, while whale and seal hunting remains important in some Arctic communities. These practices are about more than just survival; they are about preserving a way of life that has been passed down through generations.

2. Art and storytelling.
Art is a vital expression of Native identity, with each culture having its unique style. The Tlingit and Haida's elaborate totem poles, the Inupiat's ivory carvings, and the Athabascans' intricate beadwork are more than just decorations; they tell stories about ancestry, history, and spiritual beliefs.

3. Ceremony and Gathering
Traditional ceremonies remain an important part of Indigenous life. Potlatch ceremonies, held by coastal tribes such as the Tlingit and Haida, are grand feasts that

commemorate significant events such as births, marriages, and the death of elders. Dancing, drumming, and storytelling are central to these gatherings, which strengthen cultural ties within the community.

4. Spiritual beliefs.

Many Indigenous groups see themselves as land caretakers, believing that everything in nature, including animals, rivers, and mountains, has a spirit. This deep reverence for the natural world pervades their customs, from hunting rituals that honor the spirit of the animal to practices that ensure the sustainable use of resources. Connecting with Native Alaskan Culture Today.

Visitors can experience and learn about Alaska's Indigenous heritage firsthand. Cultural centers, museums, and community events provide insight into the traditions that have shaped Alaska over thousands of years.

The Alaska Native Heritage Center (Anchorage) is a great place to learn about all Alaska Native cultures. Visitors can see live performances, tour traditional homes, and hear stories directly from Indigenous storytellers.

Totem Bight State Historical Park (Ketchikan) - A site with beautifully restored totem poles that provide insight into the art and symbolism of the Tlingit and Haida cultures.

Sitka National Historical Park (Sitka) is home to ancient totem poles and a museum dedicated to the history of Alaska's Indigenous peoples, particularly their interactions with Russian colonizers.

Community Events - Dance, storytelling, and traditional games are used to celebrate Native culture at festivals such as the Fairbanks Festival of Native Arts and the Alaska Federation of Natives (AFN) Convention. Attending one of these events provides an authentic experience with Indigenous traditions.

Honoring Alaska's Indigenous Heritage.

Hiking in Alaska is more than just exploring the trails; it's about walking through lands that Indigenous peoples have inhabited, cared for, and honored for millennia. Many visitors believe that the mountains, rivers, and forests are untouched, but they are deeply connected to cultures that have thrived here for thousands of years.

6.2. The Gold Rush Period and Its Legacy

The discovery of gold in the late nineteenth century transformed Alaska from a remote wilderness to a land of opportunity, drawing thousands of fortune seekers from all over the world. The Gold Rush was more than just an economic boom; it influenced the creation of towns, trails, and trade routes that still exist today. For hikers exploring Alaska, remnants of this dramatic era can be found along historic trails, in abandoned mining camps, and in the stories that still echo in the landscape.

The Klondike Gold Rush's Impact on Alaska

Although the Klondike Gold Rush (1896-1899) is most commonly associated with Canada's Yukon Territory, Alaska was an important gateway to the goldfields. When gold was discovered in the Klondike region, prospectors needed a way to get to the remote mining sites, and many of them traveled through Alaska's rugged wilderness to do so. Skagway and Dyea became boomtowns almost overnight, serving as staging areas for stampeders making the perilous journey to the Yukon.

The demand for access resulted in the construction of infamous trails such as the Chilkoot Trail and the White Pass Trail, both of which are still hiked today. These trails were difficult, frequently covered in deep snow, and littered with abandoned supplies from exhausted travelers who couldn't carry their loads any further. Many people died during the journey due to harsh weather, avalanches, and treacherous river crossings.

As gold fever spread, discoveries in Alaska sparked other major rushes, such as the Nome Gold Rush (1899–1909) and the Fairbanks Gold Rush (1902–1911). These later discoveries helped to establish permanent settlements, transforming small camps into major towns that still exist today.

Trails and landmarks from the Gold Rush

Many trails and sites still serve as living museums of the Gold Rush era for hikers who want to experience it firsthand. These routes offer not only scenic beauty but also insight into the determination and hardships of early prospectors.

1. The Chilkoot Trail (Skagway to Yukon)

The Chilkoot Trail, perhaps the most well-known of all Gold Rush trails, served as the primary route for thousands of stampeders heading to the Klondike. This 33-mile (53-kilometer) trail, which begins in Dyea, Alaska and crosses into Canada, is now designated as a National Historic Park in the United States and a National Historic Site in Canada.

Hiking the Chilkoot Trail today is like going back in time. Along the way, you'll come across abandoned supplies, the ghost town of Sheep Camp, and the infamous Golden Stairs, where prospectors once hauled a literal ton of supplies up an icy slope to meet Canadian self-sufficiency standards. The trail is difficult, with steep sections and unpredictable weather, but those who complete it have an unforgettable historical experience.

2. White Pass Trail, Skagway

The White Pass Trail, also known as the "Dead Horse Trail" because of the thousands of pack animals that died along its path, served as an alternative route to the Klondike. This trail, unlike the Chilkoot, was designed to accommodate pack animals rather than hand-carried loads. However, the harsh terrain and brutal conditions made it equally deadly.

Today, portions of the White Pass & Yukon Route Railroad follow this historic trail, providing visitors with a scenic train ride through the rugged mountains that desperate gold seekers once climbed. While the original footpath is rarely hiked, portions of it can still be found near Skagway.

3. Nome's Golden Beaches
Unlike most gold rush towns, Nome did not require a perilous inland journey; gold was discovered on its beaches. During the Nome Gold Rush, prospectors lined the beaches, panning for gold directly in the sand. This boom transformed Nome into a wild frontier town, complete with saloons, gamblers, and fortune seekers.

Modern visitors can still try their luck at gold panning on Nome's beaches, with some areas designated for recreational prospecting. For those who are interested in history, old dredges and mining relics can be found scattered throughout the area.

4. Fairbanks and the Legacy of Felix Pedro
The interior town of Fairbanks owes much of its existence to Felix Pedro's discovery of gold in 1902. His discovery sparked the Fairbanks Gold Rush, resulting in

rapid growth of the town and the establishment of large-scale mining operations.

Today, visitors can tour Gold Dredge 8, a preserved mining dredge that demonstrates how gold was extracted in the early twentieth century. The Pedro Monument, which stands near the site of his original discovery, pays tribute to the man whose discovery helped shape Fairbanks into a major Alaskan city.

5. Independence Mine State Historic Park (Hatcher Pass). Independence Mine in Hatcher Pass, near Palmer, provides a unique opportunity to explore a well-preserved gold mine. This former gold mining complex, now a state historical park, contains abandoned buildings, old mining equipment, and interpretive signs that detail the lives of miners who worked there in the early 1900s. The surrounding mountains offer excellent hiking opportunities, making for an ideal combination of history and outdoor adventure.

Gold Rush Legacy in Alaska

The effects of the Gold Rush can still be seen throughout Alaska. While the gold rush has subsided, its legacy lives on in the form of roads, towns, and industries that arose from the mining boom. Many of Alaska's modern highways, including the Alaska Highway and the Dalton Highway, originated during these early gold-seeking expeditions.

Beyond infrastructure, Alaskan culture still embodies the spirit of adventure that defined the Gold Rush. Many residents maintain a rugged, self-sufficient lifestyle, echoing the determination of the early prospectors. Recreational gold panning remains popular, and some small-scale mining operations continue to operate in remote areas of the state.

The trails of the Gold Rush provide hikers with more than just scenic beauty; they are also historical pathways. Whether hiking the Chilkoot Trail, exploring the ruins of an old mining town, or standing atop a mountain once traversed by desperate prospectors, each step serves as a reminder of Alaska's resilience and ambition.

6.3. Natural History of Alaska.

Alaska's landscape reflects the powerful geological forces that shaped it over millions of years. From towering glaciers and active volcanoes to vast tundras and temperate rainforests, the state's natural history is marked by dramatic change and unparalleled biodiversity. Hikers see this history as more than just a backdrop; it is a living story embedded in every mountain, river, and valley. Understanding the forces that shaped Alaska allows for a greater appreciation for its natural beauty and the fragile ecosystems that exist within it.

Glaciers, Volcanoes, and Unique Ecosystems.

1. The legacy of glaciers

Alaska has the most glaciers of any state in the United States, with an estimated 100,000 glaciers covering approximately 5% of its landmass. These slow-moving ice rivers have carved deep fjords, shaped entire mountain ranges, and created some of the world's most breathtaking scenery.

During the last Ice Age, much of Alaska was covered in massive ice sheets, which gradually receded to form the valleys and coastlines that exist today. Even today, glaciers are a dominant feature of the landscape, with some still advancing and others rapidly shrinking due to climate change.

Popular glaciers for hiking and exploration are:
Exit Glacier (Kenai Fjords National Park) is one of Alaska's most accessible glaciers, with trails that allow visitors to walk along the icy surface.
Matanuska Glacier (near Anchorage) - A massive, easily accessible glacier where hikers can walk directly onto the ice.

Root Glacier (Wrangell-St. Elias National Park) is an incredible place for ice hiking, complete with deep blue crevasses and meltwater streams.
While glaciers are fascinating to see up close, they also serve as important water sources, feeding rivers and lakes that sustain Alaska's wildlife. As these glaciers

melt, they contribute to rising sea levels, affecting ecosystems in ways that scientists are still investigating.

2. Alaska's Volcanic Landscape

Volcanic activity, a dynamic and often volatile force, exists beneath Alaska's rugged terrain. The state is located along the Pacific Ring of Fire, a massive tectonic zone where earthquakes and volcanic eruptions are common. Alaska has more than 130 volcanoes, many of which are still active today.

Some of the most famous volcanic regions are:

Katmai National Park is home to *Novarupta*, the site of one of the most powerful volcanic eruptions in recorded history (1912), which reshaped the entire region and created the eerie Valley of Ten Thousand Smokes.

Mount Redoubt and Mount Augustine are active volcanoes that have erupted in recent decades, spreading ash clouds across the state.

Aniakchak Crater is a remote and rarely visited volcanic caldera with one of Alaska's wildest landscapes.

Hikers exploring volcanic regions will encounter dramatic landscapes such as hardened lava fields, deep craters, and steaming fumaroles. These areas serve as a stark reminder that powerful geological forces continue to shape Alaska.

3. The diversity of Alaska's ecosystems.

Alaska's vast size and diverse climate give rise to an incredible variety of ecosystems. From frozen tundras to lush rainforests, the state has an incredible variety of plant and animal life.

➤ The Arctic Tundra, found in northern Alaska, is a treeless landscape with harsh winters and short summers. It's home to caribou herds, Arctic foxes, and polar bears.

➤ The Boreal Forest (Taiga) - This vast coniferous forest spans the interior Alaska and is dominated by spruce, birch, and aspen trees. Wolves, moose, and grizzly bears flourish here.

➤ The coastal rainforests - These temperate rainforests are located in southeastern Alaska and are part of the larger Tongass National Forest. Bald eagles, black bears, and salmon-filled streams thrive in the towering Sitka spruce and western hemlock forests.

➤ Alaska has one of the world's longest coastlines, which supports a diverse marine ecosystem. Whales, sea otters, puffins, and seals thrive in these cold, nutrient-rich waters.

These ecosystems allow hikers to see Alaska's incredible wildlife in its natural habitat. However, given the delicate balance of these environments, responsible hiking and conservation efforts are essential.

The establishment of Alaska's national parks

Alaska is home to some of the world's most spectacular national parks, each of which preserves a unique piece of natural history. Many of these parks were established to protect fragile ecosystems, historic sites, and vast wilderness areas.

1. The Alaska National Interest Lands Conservation Act (ANILCA). One of the most significant moments in Alaska's conservation history occurred in 1980, when the United States government passed the Alaska National Interest Lands Conservation Act (ANILCA). The legislation:

➢ Established or expanded 13 national parks, preserves, and refuges.

➢ Over 104 million acres have been designated as federally protected land.

➢ Established vast wilderness areas to ensure they remain undeveloped.

➢ As a result, Alaska's national parks now cover more land than all of the other U.S. national parks combined. These parks remain among the world's most untouched and remote areas.

2. Alaska's most iconic national parks.

Each national park in Alaska tells a unique story about its natural history.

➢ Denali National Park is home to Denali (Mount McKinley), North America's highest peak. This park exemplifies the power of glacial erosion and tectonic uplift, with vast tundras, braided rivers, and an abundance of wildlife.

➢ Glacier Bay National Park – A living laboratory of glacial movement, where visitors can see tidewater glaciers calving into the sea. The region was completely covered in ice just 250 years ago, demonstrating the glaciers' rapid retreat.

➢ Wrangell-St. Elias National Park – The largest national park in the United States, with some of the highest peaks and longest glaciers in North America. The Malaspina Glacier, visible from space, flows like a frozen river into the Gulf of Alaska.

➢ Katmai National Park – Famous for the aftermath of the Novarupta eruption, which altered the landscape and created the Valley of Ten Thousand Smokes, a barren wasteland of volcanic ash and steam vents.

➢ Gates to the Arctic National Park A vast, roadless wilderness north of the Arctic Circle that protects one of the last truly untouched ecosystems on the planet.

➢ For hikers, these parks provide an unparalleled opportunity to see Alaska's natural history up close. Whether trekking across ancient glaciers, walking along volcanic craters, or witnessing the slow march of ecological succession in post-glacial landscapes, each step through these parks tells a story about the forces that shaped this wild land.

Alaska's Ever-Changing Landscape

Alaska is still evolving. Its glaciers continue to carve valleys, its volcanoes remain active, and its ecosystems adapt to changing climates. Understanding this dynamic history enhances the hiking experience by providing a deeper connection to the land and its untamed beauty. Whether standing on the edge of a glacier, climbing the slopes of a dormant volcano, or wandering through ancient forests, every hiker in Alaska contributes to the ongoing story of this extraordinary place.

6.4. Stories from the trails

Alaska has long attracted explorers, adventurers, and hikers drawn to its unspoiled wilderness and harsh conditions. Over time, some of these people have left remarkable stories of resilience, survival, and discovery. Their experiences, whether triumphant or tragic, have become part of the state's legacy, inspiring hikers from all over the world to tackle Alaska's rugged trails.

Famous Alaskan hikers and adventurers

1. John Muir: The Father of National Parks.

Although best known for his work in Yosemite, John Muir was also fascinated by Alaska. Muir first visited Glacier Bay in 1879 and was captivated by the towering ice formations and nature's raw power. He explored the area extensively, hiking across glaciers and even camping on ice floes.

Muir's descriptions of Alaska's landscapes contributed to increased awareness of the state's ecological significance. His writings influenced conservation efforts and eventually led to the establishment of Glacier Bay National Park. Hikers who follow in Muir's footsteps can now enjoy the same breathtaking scenery that inspired him to advocate for wilderness preservation.

2. *Christopher McCandless:* The Story of "Into the Wild"
Few modern adventurers are as famous—or controversial—as Christopher McCandless. His journey into the Alaskan wilderness was chronicled in Jon Krakauer's book Into the Wild, which was later made into a film.
In 1992, McCandless, a young man from Virginia, left mainstream society in search of solitude and self-reliance. He hiked into the wilderness of Denali National Park, settling near the Stampede Trail and living in an abandoned Fairbanks city bus known as "Bus 142." McCandless died tragically after approximately 113 days in the wild, most likely due to starvation and the consumption of toxic plants.

His story has sparked debate—some regard him as a naive dreamer, while others see him as a symbol of raw adventure and individuality. Regardless, his journey continues to captivate hikers and adventurers around the world. The bus, which had become a pilgrimage site for visitors, was finally removed in 2020 due to safety concerns.

3. Roman Dial: The Modern Alaskan Explorer.
Few people capture the spirit of Alaskan adventure like Roman Dial. Dial is a legendary endurance athlete, biologist, and extreme adventurer who has spent decades exploring Alaska's most remote and uncharted areas.

Dial is best known for pioneering "packrafting," a type of lightweight rafting that enables hikers to cross rivers and lakes deep in the wilderness. His expeditions frequently combine mountaineering, hiking, and river travel in novel ways that challenge modern exploration.

Cody Roman Dial, Dial's son, went missing while trekking alone in the Costa Rican jungle in 2014. His disappearance sparked a years-long search, adding another tragic and mysterious chapter to the Dial family's adventurous legacy.

For those looking for authentic backcountry adventure, Roman Dial's philosophy of lightweight travel and deep wilderness immersion provides a glimpse into the extreme side of Alaskan exploration.

4. Carl Ben Eielson, the pioneer of Alaskan backcountry travel.

Carl Ben Eielson, despite not being a traditional hiker, was instrumental in opening up Alaska's wilderness for exploration. Eielson was one of the first pilots to navigate

Alaska's harsh terrain, using aircraft to reach remote areas that were previously inaccessible.

His daring flights helped establish air routes to the Arctic, transforming how people traveled and explored Alaska. Today, hikers visiting Wrangell-St. Elias National Park and Gates of the Arctic National Park frequently rely on bush planes, an innovation pioneered by Eielson. His contributions paved the way for modern backcountry exploration.

5. Barbara Washburn is the first woman to summit Denali.
Barbara Washburn made history in 1947 as the first woman to summit Denali at a time when mountaineering was widely thought to be a male-dominated sport. She braved extreme cold and high altitudes with her husband, renowned mountaineer Bradford Washburn, to complete what was previously thought to be an impossible feat.

Barbara's ascent demonstrated that women can climb the same rugged peaks as men, paving the way for future female climbers. Today, her legacy continues to inspire hikers who face Alaska's formidable mountains.

These are just a few of the many adventurers who helped shape Alaska's hiking culture. Each story serves as a reminder that the wilderness is both breathtaking and unforgiving, demanding respect, preparation, and resilience from those who venture into it.

For modern hikers, these legends serve as both an inspiration and a lesson: Alaska is a land that rewards hard work and preparation, but it is also one of the last truly wild places on the planet. Whether you're following in John Muir's footsteps, standing where Barbara once climbed, or reflecting on Christopher McCandless's journey, every trail in Alaska holds a story waiting to be discovered.

Chapter 7

Flora and fauna Along Trails

Alaska's vast wilderness supports an incredible diversity of plant and animal life. Every trail, from the coastal rainforests of the southeast to the tundra-covered mountains of the Arctic, allows hikers to experience nature in its rawest form. The state's ecosystems range from dense boreal forests to open alpine meadows, and each supports a distinct set of wildlife.

Hiking in Alaska involves sharing the landscape with some of North America's most iconic species. Encounters with grizzly bears, moose, caribou, and wolves are possible, but they must be approached with caution and respect. Understanding the wildlife in the region is critical for both safety and conservation.

7.1. Wildlife You Might Encounter

Alaska is home to some of the most fascinating and powerful wildlife in North America. Whether you're hiking through Denali National Park, the Kenai Peninsula, or deep into Wrangell-St. Elias, these are some of the animals you might see.

1. Bears: Grizzlies and Black Bears

Bears are probably the most well-known and respected wildlife in Alaska. The state has three species:

Grizzly bears (brown bears) – Grizzlies are found all over Alaska, particularly in coastal areas, tundra, and river valleys. They can weigh over 1,000 pounds and stand over 8 feet tall on their hind legs. They are most active in the spring, summer, and fall, feeding on salmon, berries, and plants.

Black Bears – Black bears are smaller and more commonly found in forests and lower elevations; they are excellent climbers and avoid human contact.
Polar Bears - Found only in Arctic Alaska, these bears are rarely seen by hikers because they live primarily in coastal ice regions.
While bear encounters are uncommon, they necessitate caution. Carrying bear spray, making noise while hiking, and properly storing food are all important ways to avoid conflicts.

2. Moose
The Giants of the Forest Moose are the largest members of the deer family, standing over six feet tall and weighing up to 1,500 pounds. They are frequently seen near wetlands, lakes, and forested trails, particularly in Denali, Chugach State Park, and the Kenai Peninsula.
Moose, despite their calm appearance, can be unpredictable and aggressive, particularly during calving season (spring) when mothers protect their young.
Rut season (fall) is when bulls become more territorial.

Hikers should never approach a moose because it can charge unexpectedly. If a moose blocks the trail, stay at a safe distance until it moves on.

3. Wolves - The elusive predators.

Wolves live in Alaska's remote wilderness areas, particularly Denali, Wrangell-St. Elias, and the Arctic. While they are rarely seen by hikers, their tracks and distant howls can occasionally be heard in open tundra or dense forests.

Wolves are extremely intelligent and typically avoid human interaction. In the unlikely event of an encounter, never run; instead, stand tall, make eye contact, and slowly back away.

4. Caribou, the Great Migrators

Caribou herds travel across Alaska's tundra and open landscapes, frequently seen in Denali National Park, the Arctic National Wildlife Refuge, and Wrangell-St. Elias. These animals, which are related to reindeer, are notable for their seasonal migrations and distinctive antlers.

Hikers who are fortunate enough to witness a herd moving across the land will see one of nature's most spectacular sights.

5. Dall Sheep – The High Climbers

Dall sheep are frequently spotted in alpine areas, gracefully navigating rocky ridges in Denali, Chugach, and the Talkeetna Mountains. These white-coated animals are excellent climbers, using their powerful hooves to scale cliffs and avoid predators such as wolves. If you're hiking at higher elevations, keep an eye on the ridgelines; you might see a small herd silhouetted against the sky.

6. Bald Eagles – The Majestic Hunters

The bald eagle, a symbol of America's wild spirit, is found throughout Alaska, particularly along coastlines, rivers, and lakes. They are frequently spotted soaring above Glacier Bay, the Kenai Fjords, and the Inside Passage, hunting for fish with their sharp talons.

Bald eagles are a breathtaking sight for hikers, especially near salmon-rich waters where they congregate in droves.

7. Smaller Mammals: Foxes, Lynx, and Marmots.

Red Foxes - Quick and curious, foxes roam the forests and tundra, frequently darting across open meadows.

Lynx - These elusive wildcats, distinguished by their tufted ears, are rarely seen but live in dense forests throughout Alaska.

Marmots and Arctic Ground Squirrels - These small, burrowing mammals are common in alpine meadows, often basking on rocks or chirping to alert predators.

Tips for Hiking Safely Around Wildlife Exploring Alaska's wildlife can be exciting, but it also poses risks.

Following proper safety guidelines results in a safe and enjoyable hiking experience.

1. Bear Safety.

➢ Always carry bear spray and understand how to use it.

➢ Make noise while hiking, particularly in dense vegetation or near rivers.

➢ When camping, make sure to store food in bear-proof containers or use bear hangs.

➢ If you encounter a bear, don't run; instead, stand your ground and slowly back away.

2. Moose Safety.

➢ Never approach a moose, even if it appears calm.

➢ If a moose charges, run and hide behind a tree or large object.

➢ Avoid hiking through dense brush where moose could be hiding.

3. General Wildlife Safety.

➢ Maintain a safe distance from all animals and use binoculars or a zoom lens instead of approaching.

➢ Never feed wildlife because it disrupts their natural behavior and can lead to dangerous situations.

➢ Be aware of seasonal changes: Animals behave differently during breeding, migration, and winter.

➢ A land of wild encounters.

➤ Hiking in Alaska provides the opportunity to see some of the most extraordinary wildlife on the planet. Every trail has the potential to provide a close encounter with nature, whether it's a bald eagle soaring overhead, a herd of caribou crossing the tundra, or a bear fishing for salmon in a rushing river.

7.2. Wildflowers, trees, and vegetation.

Alaska's trails are adorned with a diverse array of plant life, with each species telling a story of resilience and adaptation. The flora here not only adds to the scenic beauty but also serves an important role in the ecosystem by supporting wildlife and maintaining ecological balance.

Notable Flora in the Alaskan Wilderness

As one travels through the diverse landscapes of Alaska, several plant species stand out:

Fireweed (Chamerion angustifolium): This tall, elegant plant is adorned with vibrant pink to purple petals that unfold gradually as summer progresses. Fireweed's appearance is frequently used as a season indicator, with locals claiming that summer is over when the top blooms reach the flower's tip.citeturn0search2

Forget-Me-Not (Myosotis alpestris): The forget-me-not is a small but striking wildflower found in Alaska. This flower, with its delicate, sky-blue petals and bright yellow center, is both a symbol of remembrance and a state emblem. In 1949, Alaska officially adopted the name "forget-me-not" as its state flower (citeturn0search2.

Sitka Spruce (Picea sitchensis): The Sitka spruce is a towering conifer that can grow to be 225 feet tall and dominates coastal forests. Its wood has historically been valuable to indigenous communities and the timber industry.citeturn0search14

Arctic Lupine (Lupinus arcticus): With its vibrant blue to purple flower spikes, the Arctic lupine thrives in well-drained soils and open areas, adding color to the tundra and meadows.citeturn0search6

Alaska Wild Rose (Rosa acicularis): This hardy shrub with fragrant pink flowers is commonly found along forest edges and in open fields. Its bright red rose hips provide a vital food source for wildlife during the winter.citeturn0search6 These species, among others, demonstrate the botanical diversity that hikers can enjoy on Alaska's trails.

Seasonal Flowers and Viewing Tips
The blooming seasons in Alaska are brief but spectacular, thanks to the state's unique climate and extended daylight hours during the summer. To optimize the experience:

➢ Spring (May to June): As temperatures rise, higher elevations and coastal areas bloom. Early bloomers include Western Columbine and Small-flowered Paintbrush.

➤ Summer (July–August): Alpine meadows and tundra regions reach their peak flowering period. This is the best time to see the colorful displays of Fireweed, Arctic Lupine, and the state flower, Forget-Me-Not.

➤ Fall (September): As temperatures drop, many plants set seed, and the foliage of shrubs such as Dwarf Birch and Willows turns golden, providing a unique form of beauty. For the optimal viewing experience:

➤ Timing: Lan hikes during peak bloom periods, keeping in mind that higher elevations bloom later due to remaining snow.

➤ Location: Look up specific trails known for their floral displays. Denali National Park and the Kenai Peninsula are known for their diverse plant life.

➤ Respect: Follow marked trails to protect fragile plant communities. Avoid picking wildflowers to protect them for future generations and allow them to complete their life cycles. Aligning hiking plans with these seasonal cues allows one to fully immerse oneself in Alaska's botanical wonders.

7.3. Conservation efforts

The pristine beauty of Alaska's trails and ecosystems is the result of dedicated conservation efforts to protect this natural heritage for future generations.

Protecting Alaska's Trails and Ecosystems.
Several organizations and initiatives are at the forefront
of protecting Alaska's environment.

➤ Alaska Conservation Foundation: This organization
works to build climate resilience and protect public
lands and waters, ensuring that Alaska's unparalleled
natural heritage is preserved.

➤ The Center for Alaskan Coastal Studies conserves
and stewards over 800 acres of critical wildlife habitat
across Kachemak Bay, serving as a model for land
management and ecological monitoring efforts aimed
at supporting healthy communities where people and
wildlife can coexist.

➤ The Alaska Wildlife Alliance is dedicated to
protecting Alaska's wildlife through citizen
mobilization, advocacy, and education, and it plays an
important role in conservation.citeturn0search13
These organizations, among others, work tirelessly
to combat issues such as habitat degradation, climate
change, and unsustainable development.

How Hikers Can Help.
Hikers, as trail stewards, play an important role in
conservation.
Practice Leave No Trace Principles: remove all trash,
reduce campfire impact, and respect wildlife to preserve
the trails' natural integrity.
Stay on designated paths to prevent soil erosion and
protect sensitive vegetation.

Participate in Local Conservation Programs: Get involved with organizations like the Student Conservation Association, which has crews working to improve public lands throughout Alaska.

Educate Yourself and Others: Understanding the local ecosystems and the significance of conservation can motivate responsible behavior and advocacy.

Chapter 8

Dining, drinking, and relaxing.

8.1. Best Places to Eat Following a Long Hike

After a rewarding hike through Alaska's breathtaking landscapes, finding the ideal spot to relax and eat a hearty meal is critical. Here are some local favorites that provide delicious food and a welcoming environment:

1. The Bake Shop, located in Girdwood, is known for its sourdough pancakes and bottomless soup. The cozy atmosphere and friendly service make it an ideal place to relax after exploring the nearby trails.

2. Jack Sprat, located in Girdwood, offers a diverse menu to accommodate various dietary preferences. Their dishes are made with fresh, local ingredients, resulting in a satisfying dining experience in a relaxed atmosphere.

3. Glacier Brewhouse: Located in Anchorage, Glacier Brewhouse is popular among both locals and visitors. The restaurant has a large, rustic dining area with a central fireplace that creates a warm and welcoming atmosphere. They serve fresh seafood and meats, along with a selection of homemade beers. Before or after your meal, you can see the brewing equipment through a glass wall.

4. Snow City Café, located in downtown Anchorage, is well-known for its breakfast offerings. Locals praise their egg scrambles, omelets, and made-from-scratch bakery items. Popular combinations include eggs Benedict with sockeye salmon cakes and hot oatmeal topped with homemade granola and blueberries.

5. The Crow's Nest Restaurant, located atop Hotel Captain Cook in Anchorage, serves a mix of French and New American cuisine. His AAA Four-Diamond fine dining restaurant offers breathtaking views of downtown Anchorage, the Chugach Mountains, and Cook Inlet. Washes uses locally sourced ingredients such as venison loin and Bering Sea king crab legs.

6. Seven Glaciers Restaurant, located 2,300 feet above sea level on Mount Alyeska in Girdwood, is one of only three AAA Four-Diamond restaurants in Alaska. The dining experience begins with a tram ride high above the treetops, followed by an elevator lift to a dining room that reflects the colors of alpenglow and glacial ice. The menu offers innovative cuisine with panoramic views.

7. Tidewater Tap House: Tidewater Taphouse, located in Seward, serves local craft beers, delicious food, and beautiful water views. The cozy interior has colorful wood-planked walls adorned with nautical statues and bronze artifacts from ships. The 16-foot glass garage door opens onto a large outdoor patio complete with picnic tables and Adirondack chairs.

8. Big Daddy's BBQ, located in Fairbanks, is a must-visit for barbecue lovers. This restaurant, featured on "Diners, Drive-Ins, and Dives," serves delicious barbecue, including brisket and a variety of side dishes. While it may not appear impressive from the outside, the food is amazing.

8.2 Best Drinks: Coffee, Beer, and Alaskan Brews

After a long day of hiking, a refreshing beverage can be the ideal way to unwind. Alaska's diverse offerings cater to a variety of tastes, ranging from robust coffees to unique local brews.

Coffee

Alaska's coffee culture is rich and diverse, with many local establishments serving excellent brews. Here are some famous coffee shops to consider:

1. Kaladi Brothers Coffee.
Kaladi Brothers Coffee, founded in 1986, has grown from a small coffee cart to a popular local roaster. They provide a variety of blends and single-origin coffees, all roasted in Anchorage. Their dedication to quality and community makes them a must-see for coffee lovers.

2. The Grind, located in the heart of Girdwood, is renowned for its welcoming atmosphere and exceptional coffee. It's an excellent place to unwind and enjoy a warm beverage after a day on the trails.

3. Black Cup Coffee Company. Black Cup Coffee Co., which has multiple locations in Anchorage, provides a

comfortable atmosphere as well as a variety of high-quality coffees. Their commitment to sustainability and community engagement makes them an outstanding choice.

Beer and Alaskan Breweries

Alaska's craft beer scene is thriving, with numerous breweries serving a variety of styles. Here are a few notable breweries to visit:

1. Anchorage Brewing Company is known for their innovative beers, such as barrel-aged and sour ales. Their tasting room provides a cozy setting in which to sample their unique creations.

2. Seward Brewing Company, located in Seward, produces a variety of craft beers on-site. The menu includes dishes that complement their beers, making it an ideal spot to unwind after a day of exploring.

3. Homer Brewing Company: A popular local hangout in Homer. They serve handcrafted ales and lagers made with high-quality ingredients, ideal for winding down after a day of adventure. Whether you're looking for a soothing drink or a place to unwind, Alaska's diverse offerings ensure a satisfying conclusion to your hiking adventures.

After exploring Alaska's rugged trails, it's critical to find ways to relax and recharge. The state provides a variety of options, ranging from relaxing hot springs to exciting outdoor activities, allowing you to unwind in harmony with nature.

Spas & Hot Springs
Alaska's geothermal activity has produced natural hot springs, which are ideal for relaxing after a long day.

Chena Hot Springs Resort
Chena Hot Springs Resort, about 60 miles northeast of Fairbanks, is known for its natural geothermal waters. Visitors can relax in the warm, mineral-rich waters of Rock Lake, which is located in the Alaskan wilderness. The resort also has an indoor pool and hot tubs filled with chlorinated geothermal water, providing a safe and comfortable experience. Aside from soaking, guests can visit the Aurora Ice Museum, get massages, and engage in other recreational activities.

Alyeska Nordic Spa.
The Alyeska Nordic Spa, located in Girdwood's Chugach Mountains, provides a modern alpine sanctuary. This 50,000-square-foot spa offers a hydrotherapy experience with a network of hot, warm, and cold pools, as well as steam rooms and saunas, all set against the backdrop of a northern rainforest. The spa encourages relaxation

through the use of hydrotherapy, allowing guests to unwind and rejuvenate in a peaceful setting.

Manley Hot Springs

Manley Hot Springs, located approximately 150 miles west of Fairbanks, provides a more rustic and secluded experience. The resort offers lodging, camping, and access to a hot spring-fed pool. It's ideal for those looking for peace away from the crowds.

Outdoor Recreation

Alaska's diverse landscapes provide numerous opportunities for active relaxation.

➢ Wildlife Viewing: Many areas offer opportunities to observe Alaska's unique wildlife, such as bears, moose, and various bird species.

➢ Fishing: With its abundant rivers and lakes, fishing is a popular pastime that provides both relaxation and the thrill of the catch.

➢ Kayaking and canoeing: Exploring Alaska's waterways provides a peaceful connection with nature, whether you're paddling through tranquil lakes or along coastal shores.

Engaging in these activities not only helps you relax but also gives you a better understanding of Alaska's natural beauty.

8.4 Food to Pack for Alaska Trails

Proper nutrition is essential when going on hikes in Alaska. Packing the right foods helps to maintain energy levels and promotes overall well-being during your adventure.

Quick Energy Foods

➢ Choose lightweight, non-perishable items that offer a quick energy boost:

➢ Trail mix: Nuts, dried fruits, and seeds provide a balanced source of carbohydrates, healthy fats, and proteins.

➢ Energy Bars: Choose low-sugar, high-protein bars to keep your energy levels stable without causing spikes and crashes.

➢ Jerky: Beef or turkey jerky is a portable source of protein that promotes muscle repair and satiety.

➢ Dried fruits such as raisins, apricots, and mangoes provide natural sugars for quick energy and are easy to pack.

➢ Nuts and Seeds: Almonds, walnuts, and sunflower seeds are high in healthy fats and proteins, helping you stay full and energized.

Cooking for Backcountry

➢ For longer hikes or overnight trips, consider meals that are simple to prepare.

➢ Instant oatmeal: A light breakfast option that uses only hot water and can be topped with dried fruits or nuts.

➢ Dehydrated Meals: Commercially available dehydrated meals are convenient, require little preparation, and provide balanced nutrition.

➢ Ramen noodles are lightweight and quick to cook. They can be combined with dehydrated vegetables or protein sources to make a more substantial meal.

➢ Tortillas with Nut Butter: A non-perishable option that contains carbohydrates and healthy fats, making it an ideal snack or meal.

➢ Canned fish, such as tuna or salmon, contains protein and healthy fats; choose vacuum-sealed pouches to lose weight.

Chapter 9

Events, Festivals, and Activities

9.1. Alaskan Trail Races and Events

Alaska is a land of endurance, both in terms of natural landscapes and the spirit of those who travel through it. Alaska's vast wilderness, extreme weather, and rugged terrain have long challenged adventurers, and for many, the best way to embrace that challenge is to compete in one of the state's legendary trail races or hiking celebrations. From world-famous sled dog races to grueling ultra-marathons and local community treks, these events demonstrate people's tenacity, skill, and deep connection to Alaska's wilderness.

Iditarod

No discussion of Alaskan endurance events is complete without mentioning the Iditarod Trail Sled Dog Race. While not a traditional hiking event, the Iditarod captures the essence of human and animal endurance in the frozen wilderness. Every March, mushers and their sled dog teams travel 1,000 miles from Anchorage to Nome, braving snowstorms, subzero temperatures, and some of North America's most difficult terrain.

The trail itself follows former mail and supply routes used by Alaska Natives and early settlers. Today, the Iditarod is more than just a race; it's a celebration of survival, adventure, and the strong bond between mushers and dogs. Visitors to Alaska during this time can witness the ceremonial start in Anchorage, where thousands gather to cheer on the teams as they march through the snow-covered streets. Along the route, checkpoints in remote villages provide glimpses into traditional Alaskan life, where hospitality and resilience have been essential for centuries.

While the Iditarod is only for dog sled teams, portions of the historic Iditarod Trail are open to hikers, allowing them to follow in the footsteps of previous adventurers. Sections of the trail, especially in the summer, reveal breathtaking mountain views, frozen rivers, and the vast solitude of the Alaskan backcountry.

Mount Marathon Race
For those looking to test their physical limits on foot, the Mount Marathon Race in Seward is one of Alaska's most punishing and renowned trail races. This annual event, held on July 4th, is a brutal but exhilarating climb up and down Mount Marathon, a peak that rises steeply from the coastal town of Seward. Runners climb 3,000 feet in just over a mile, scrambling over rocky terrain, dodging loose scree, and battling exhaustion before descending at breakneck speed.

This race has been a part of Seward's Independence Day celebrations for more than a century, dating back to a barroom bet in 1915. Today, it draws elite trail runners, adventurous locals, and even fearless first-timers eager to take on the challenge. For spectators, the event is as exciting to watch as it is to participate in. The entire town comes alive with celebrations, street fairs, and local seafood feasts, providing an unforgettable Alaskan experience.

Equinox Marathon & Ultramarathon

The Equinox Marathon and Ultramarathon in Fairbanks is one of Alaska's premier long-distance running events, covering miles of scenic wilderness. This race, held in September, follows a spectacular course through birch forests, mountain ridges, and rolling tundra, with breathtaking fall foliage and crisp autumn air. The marathon starts and ends at the University of Alaska Fairbanks, climbing to the top of Ester Dome before returning to town.

While it is a running event, many participants choose to hike portions of the course, enjoying the challenge at a slower pace while taking in the breathtaking Alaskan scenery. The race is known for its welcoming and inclusive atmosphere, which attracts both elite athletes and casual outdoor enthusiasts looking to explore Alaska's backcountry on foot.

Crow Pass Crossing

For those seeking a trail race that feels more like an adventure expedition, the Crow Pass Crossing is one of Alaska's most difficult wilderness challenges. This 22-

mile backcountry race from Girdwood to Eagle River requires participants to navigate rough mountain terrain, cross rivers, and pass through bear country without the use of marked trails or support stations.

The race follows the historic Iditarod supply route through Chugach State Park, which has some of the most rugged and spectacular scenery in the state. Participants must be completely self-sufficient, with bear spray, survival gear, and enough food and water to make it through the remote wilderness. The reward for completing this brutal trek is an unforgettable journey through Alaska's untouched landscapes, as well as the sheer satisfaction of winning one of the state's most punishing races.

Hiking and Community Trekking Events.

Not every hiking event in Alaska focuses on speed and endurance. Many communities hold annual trekking festivals to celebrate Alaska's breathtaking trails in a more relaxed and social atmosphere. The Anchorage RunFest, for example, offers a variety of distances for people of all fitness levels, as well as scenic hikes through coastal trails and woodland parks.

Similarly, the Kenai Peninsula Hiking Festival encourages visitors to explore the region's breathtaking trails through guided hikes, educational talks, and cultural presentations by local Indigenous communities. This event emphasizes the importance of preserving

Alaska's natural beauty while allowing hikers of all skill levels to explore its pristine wilderness.

Why These Events Matter

Beyond the physical challenge, Alaska's trail races and hiking events provide an opportunity to connect with the land, culture, and history of the state. The legendary endurance of the Iditarod, the fierce determination of the Mount Marathon Race, and the breathtaking solitude of the Crow Pass Crossing all highlight Alaska's spirit of adventure.

9.2. Wildlife Viewing Opportunities

Alaska's vast wilderness is home to some of North America's most incredible wildlife, making it an ideal destination for nature lovers. From the towering peaks of Denali to the icy waters of Glacier Bay, each region provides unique opportunities to observe animals in their natural environment. Wildlife viewing in Alaska is an unforgettable experience, whether it's watching whales breach off the coast, spotting grizzly bears in a remote valley, or hearing migratory bird calls.

Whale Watching

Few things compare to seeing a humpback whale emerge from the depths, its massive body breaking through the surface and crashing back into the water with a thunderous splash. Alaska's nutrient-rich coastal waters attract a variety of whale species, including humpback, gray, orca, and minke whales. The best time to see whales is between May and September, when they migrate through the region's fjords and bays.

Popular whale-watching destinations include:
Humpback whales are frequently spotted in the waters of Auke Bay and Stephens Passage. Many tours depart from Juneau, providing guided boat trips that increase the chances of seeing these gentle giants.

Humpbacks, orcas, and fin whales frequent Kenai Fjords National Park due to the nutrient-rich waters of the Gulf of Alaska. Boat tours from Seward offer breathtaking views of glaciers while keeping a lookout for marine life.

Prince William Sound - This sheltered coastal area is home to playful sea otters, harbor seals, and porpoises, as well as excellent whale-watching opportunities.

Icy Strait Point - This remote area near Hoonah is one of the best places in the world to see humpback whales feeding with bubble nets, a coordinated hunting technique.

Many guided tours operate throughout the summer, allowing visitors to see whales up close while learning about their behaviors and migration patterns.

Birdwatching: A Haven for Avid Birders
Alaska is home to more than 500 bird species, making it an ideal destination for bird watchers. Birdwatching in Alaska is both diverse and rewarding, with bald eagles

soaring over coastal cliffs, puffins nesting on rocky islands, and sandhill cranes gathering in wetlands.

Key birdwatching destinations include:

Potter Marsh (Anchorage) is a birdwatcher's paradise, with easy boardwalk access to see swans, geese, and shorebirds.

➢ St. Paul Island (Pribilof Islands) is one of the best places to see rare seabirds like tufted puffins and red-faced cormorants.

➢ Chilkat Bald Eagle Preserve (Haines) - In the fall, thousands of bald eagles congregate along the Chilkat River, providing an incredible sight for photographers and wildlife enthusiasts.

➢ Copper River Delta - This vast wetland is one of the world's largest shorebird staging areas, with millions of birds stopping by during migration.

➢ Those interested in learning more about Alaska's avian species can take advantage of numerous birding tours and guided hikes.

Bear Viewing.

Alaska has some of the world's largest brown and black bear populations. Seeing these magnificent animals in their natural habitat is a highlight of any trip, but you must do so safely and from a distance.

➢ Top bear-viewing spots include Katmai National Park (Brooks Falls), known for its annual salmon run, where brown bears gather to catch fish mid-leap.

- Lake Clark National Park provides remote bear-viewing opportunities amidst stunning landscapes.
- Denali National Park - Bears can occasionally be seen roaming the park's vast tundra landscapes, often looking for food.
- Admiralty Island (Fortress of the Bears) has one of the highest concentrations of brown bears in the world.
- Guided bear-viewing tours offer a safe and ethical way to see these animals up close while respecting their natural environment.

9.3 Photography Opportunities.

Alaska's dramatic landscapes, abundant wildlife, and vibrant seasonal changes make it a photographer's dream destination. Whether capturing the first light on a glacier-covered peak or photographing a bald eagle in flight, the possibilities for breathtaking photography are limitless.

Top Locations for Sunrise and Sunset Photography.

- Denali National Park - The golden hour illuminates Denali's towering peak, resulting in a breathtaking scene.
- Homer Spit - The sunset over Kachemak Bay illuminates the sky with brilliant colors that reflect off the water.
- Morning light casts a soft glow over Mendenhall Glacier, a stunning blue ice formation.

➤ Glacier Bay National Park - The early morning mist and reflections in the fjords create stunning compositions.

Wildlife Photography Hotspots
➤ Kodiak Island is ideal for capturing brown bears in their natural habitat.
➤ Kenai Fjords - A great place to photograph puffins, seals, and whales against the backdrop of towering glaciers.
➤ Haines (Chilkat Bald Eagle Preserve) is ideal for capturing majestic bald eagles in action.
➤ Photographers traveling to Alaska should pack a good zoom lens for wildlife shots, a wide-angle lens for landscapes, and plenty of memory cards to store their images.

9.4 Summer and Winter Hiking Activities.

Alaska's hiking opportunities vary dramatically with the seasons, providing unique experiences all year.

Summer Hiking: Long Days, Endless Trails

Summer is the most popular season for hiking in Alaska, with mild temperatures, snow-free trails, and nearly 24 hours of daylight in some areas. This season provides the best access to national parks, alpine ridges, and glacier trails.
➤ Popular Summer Hikes: Harding Icefield Trail offers breathtaking views of an ancient icefield.

- ➢ Flattop Mountain is a quick but rewarding hike near Anchorage that offers panoramic views of the city and the mountains.
- ➢ Kesugi Ridge offers breathtaking views of Denali and the surrounding tundra.
- ➢ Summer is also the best time for backcountry hiking, as it allows you to camp under the midnight sun and explore remote areas that are inaccessible in winter.

Winter Hiking: A Different Type of Adventure

- ➢ While winter brings challenges such as subzero temperatures and limited daylight, it also provides a completely different perspective on Alaska's landscapes. Winter hiking is a magical experience with snow-covered forests, frozen waterfalls, and the opportunity to see the Northern Lights.
- ➢ Popular Winter Hikes: Eagle River Nature Center Trails - Ideal for spotting moose and enjoying peaceful, snowy scenery.
- ➢ Matanuska Glacier - Ice trekking is an exciting activity that allows hikers to explore deep crevasses and blue ice caves.
- ➢ The Chena Hot Springs Trails offer a rewarding hike followed by a relaxing soak in natural hot springs.

Dress in layers, wear proper insulated boots, and bring ice-resistant gear like trekking poles and crampons.

Chapter 10

Sustainability and Leave No Trace

Alaska's landscapes are still some of the most pristine in the world, but keeping them that way requires responsible exploration. Every visitor contributes to environmental protection, whether they trek across tundra, camp near glaciers, or navigate dense forests. Understanding sustainable outdoor practices ensures that future generations can enjoy the same pristine wilderness.

10.1. Leave No Trace. Principles for Alaskan Hikers. The Leave No Trace (LNT) philosophy is critical for preserving Alaska's wilderness areas. These principles offer practical guidelines for reducing human impact while hiking, camping, and enjoying nature.

➤ Plan and prepare. The Alaskan experience includes harsh weather, remote locations, and encounters with wildlife. Checking forecasts, bringing appropriate equipment, and being familiar with park regulations all help to prevent unnecessary environmental disturbances.

➤ Travel and camp on durable surfaces. Following marked trails and established campsites reduces erosion and protects fragile vegetation. Alpine tundra, for example, requires decades to recover from damage.

- ➤ Dispose of Waste Properly – "Pack it in, pack it out" is a fundamental rule. All trash, leftover food, and biodegradable waste should be carried out. In the backcountry, human waste must be buried at least 6 inches deep or packed out in designated areas.
- ➤ Leave What You Find – Rocks, plants, and historical artifacts should remain untouched. Removing them disrupts the ecosystem and diminishes the experience for others.
- ➤ Minimize Campfire Impact – Open fires can scar the land, especially in tundra regions where organic material burns slowly. Using a camp stove is the best alternative. If fires are allowed, they should be kept small and only use dead wood found on the ground.
- ➤ Respect Wildlife – Observing animals from a distance keeps both people and wildlife safe. Feeding wild animals, even unintentionally, can alter their behavior and lead to dangerous interactions.
- ➤ Be considerate of other visitors. Alaska's trails draw hikers, photographers, and nature lovers seeking solitude. Maintaining low noise levels and yielding to uphill travelers ensures a positive experience for all.
- ➤ Applying these principles helps to keep the balance between exploration and conservation.

10.2 Environmentally Friendly Practices in Alaska.

Sustainability entails more than just reducing impact; it also entails making deliberate decisions that help conservation efforts. Hikers can reduce their footprint by making thoughtful decisions when it comes to gear, transportation, and accommodations.

➢ Sustainable Hiking and Camping - Reusable water bottles, biodegradable soap, and solar-powered chargers reduce waste and pollution. Lightweight gear made from recycled materials reduces the need for new resources. Choosing eco-certified lodges or campgrounds that use environmentally friendly practices helps to promote sustainability.

➢ Ethical Wildlife Viewing – Instead of using motorized boats or aircraft for wildlife tours, opting for silent, non-intrusive alternatives like kayaking or hiking ensures a lower impact on habitats. Responsible tour operators follow ethical guidelines that prioritize animal welfare.

➢ Eco-Friendly Travel Choices – When compared to driving alone, public transportation, shuttle services, and group tours emit less carbon. Carpooling with other hikers also reduces environmental impact. In some areas, biking is a viable option for accessing trails.

➢ Supporting conservation efforts - Many Alaskan parks and wildlife reserves depend on visitor contributions. Donating to conservation organizations, volunteering for trail maintenance programs, or participating in clean-up events are excellent ways to give back.

10.3. Protecting Alaska's Wilderness

Alaska's vast wilderness is among the most untouched and ecologically significant landscapes in the world. Its national parks, remote trails, and diverse wildlife depend on ongoing conservation efforts to counteract climate change, habitat destruction, and human impact. While state and federal organizations lead large-scale initiatives, individual hikers also play a vital role in protecting Alaska's wild spaces.

The Importance of Conservation in Alaska

Alaska's ecosystems are delicate, and even small disturbances can have long-lasting effects. Glaciers are retreating at an unprecedented rate, tundra landscapes are slow to recover from damage, and wildlife is increasingly threatened by habitat loss. Many trails pass through protected areas where conservation laws protect the environment. Understanding these efforts facilitates responsible hiking and conservation efforts.

Some key conservation areas are:

Denali National Park and Preserve – Denali's backcountry, a world-renowned habitat for wildlife such as grizzly bears, wolves, and caribou, is largely undeveloped and subject to strict regulations to preserve its natural integrity.

Gates of the Arctic National Park - This remote, roadless park preserves some of North America's last true wilderness. Conservation efforts are centered on protecting migratory routes and indigenous lands.

Kenai Fjords National Park, home to the famous Harding Icefield, experiences significant glacial melting. Research and restoration projects aim to slow the loss of ice and protect marine life in surrounding waters.

Tongass National Forest - The United States' largest national forest, this temperate rainforest serves as a critical habitat for bears, bald eagles, and salmon. Conservation programs aim to prevent deforestation and promote sustainable fishing practices.

How Hikers Can Help Conservation Efforts

Even as a visitor, there are many ways to contribute to conservation and ensure Alaska's trails remain pristine for future generations.

➢ Respect the Park Guidelines - Many protected areas have strict rules regarding camping, trail use, and wildlife interactions. Following these guidelines reduces unintentional harm to ecosystems.

➢ Stay on Marked Trails. Venturing off-trail can damage fragile plant life, cause erosion, and disturb animal habitats. Sticking to designated paths minimizes long-term damage.

➢ Join Conservation Programs: Several organizations provide volunteer opportunities for trail maintenance, habitat restoration, and wildlife monitoring. Programs such as the Alaska Conservation Foundation and National Park Service Volunteer Programs allow hikers to contribute to preservation efforts.

➢ Reduce Your Carbon Footprint – Choosing eco-friendly transportation, minimizing waste, and supporting sustainable businesses all contribute to the health of Alaska's environment. Opting for non-motorized exploration, like kayaking or backpacking instead of boat or helicopter tours, also reduces environmental impact.

➢ Support Ethical Tourism - Many tour operators and lodges use sustainable practices that prioritize conservation. Researching and selecting companies that follow responsible travel guidelines helps fund environmental protection.

➢ Participate in Leave No Trace Initiatives. Some hiking groups organize clean-up events and awareness campaigns to promote responsible outdoor ethics. Participating in these initiatives helps educate others and protect Alaska's wild spaces.

Alaska's Future Depends on Conservation

Alaska's wilderness is one of the last great frontiers, but it remains under constant pressure from climate change, tourism, and industrial development. While national parks and conservation groups work tirelessly to protect these landscapes, hikers and outdoor enthusiasts have an equally important responsibility. By hiking mindfully, supporting conservation efforts, and spreading awareness, visitors can ensure that Alaska's untamed beauty remains unspoiled for generations to come.

Chapter 11

Emergency Contacts

Alaska's remote wilderness is breathtakingly beautiful, but it also poses unique challenges and risks to hikers. The vast distances, unpredictable weather, and limited access to emergency services make preparation crucial. Knowing who to contact in case of an emergency can make all the difference.

National and State Park Emergency Services

Most of Alaska's national and state parks have ranger stations or visitor centers where hikers can seek help. However, due to the state's sheer size, not all areas have immediate ranger presence. Some remote areas require satellite communication or emergency beacons to request help. Here are the main emergency contacts for some of Alaska's most popular parks:

Denali National Park and Preserve
➢ Emergency Dispatch: (907) 683-9555 Park Headquarters: (907) 683-2294
Nearest Medical Facility
➢ Emergency Services: Call 911 (local dispatch will coordinate the response).
➢ Seward Ranger Station: (907) 422-0500.

Closest Medical Facility: Providence Seward Medical Center, Seward, AK Wrangell-St. Elias National Park & Preserve

> Emergency Contact: (907) 822-5234 Park Headquarters: (907) 822-7250 Closest Medical Facility: Cross Road Medical Center, Glennallen, AK Glacier Bay National Park

> Emergency Response: (907) 697-2230 Park Visitor Center: (907) 697-2661 Closest Medical Facility: Bartlett Regional Hospital, Juneau, AK Chugach State Park

> Alaska State Troopers (for search and rescue): (907) 428-7200 Anchorage Park Office: (907) 345-5014

> Closest Medical Facility: Providence Alaska Medical Center, Anchorage, AK

How to Call for Help in Remote Areas.
In many parts of Alaska, cell service is unreliable or nonexistent. To prepare for emergencies in these areas, hikers should consider the following:

> Carrying a Satellite Messenger or Personal Locator Beacon (PLB) – Devices like the Garmin inReach or SPOT allow users to send SOS signals with GPS coordinates.

> Using a VHF Radio – Some areas, especially coastal and marine trails, have emergency channels monitored by the U.S. Coast Guard.

> Leaving a Detailed Itinerary – Before heading into the backcountry, hikers should inform a trusted

person about their route, expected return time, and emergency plan.

Search and Rescue in Alaska

➢ Alaska has limited search and rescue (SAR) teams, and response times can vary depending on weather conditions and location. SAR efforts are usually coordinated by Alaska State Troopers, the primary agency for search and rescue outside national parks. Call 911 or the nearest trooper station for assistance.

➢ National Park Service (NPS) Rescue Teams – Available in parks like Denali, but only in areas with ranger coverage.

➢ Local Volunteer Rescue Groups – Organizations like the Alaska Mountain Rescue Group (AMRG) provide SAR services in certain regions.

Medical Assistance and Air Evacuation

In critical emergencies, LifeMed Alaska and Guardian Flight offer medical air evacuation services. However, these services can be costly, so purchasing emergency evacuation insurance is highly recommended for those venturing into remote areas.

Final Tips for Emergency Preparedness

Always carry a first-aid kit and know basic wilderness first aid.

Before you begin your hike, check the weather forecast and park conditions.

If you become lost, remain in your current location and make yourself visible to rescuers.

Avoid taking unnecessary risks—help may be hours or even days away in some areas.

11.2 Common Hiking Hazards: How to Avoid Them

Dealing with Dangerous Wildlife, Weather, and Terrain Hiking in Alaska offers breathtaking scenery, but the state's rugged wilderness also poses significant hazards. Hikers must be prepared to face a variety of challenges, including unpredictable weather, encounters with large wildlife, and difficult terrain. Understanding these dangers and knowing how to respond can help ensure a safe and enjoyable adventure.

Wildlife Hazards and Safety Measures

Alaska is home to an array of wildlife, including some of North America's largest and most powerful animals. While sightings can be thrilling, improper behavior can lead to dangerous encounters.

➢ Bears (Grizzlies and Black Bears): Avoid surprising a bear. Make noise while hiking, especially in densely vegetated areas or near rivers. Calling out, clapping, or using bear bells will alert bears to your presence.

➢ Store food properly – When camping, use bear-proof containers or hang food from a tree at least 100 yards from your sleeping area.

➢ Carry bear spray – This is the most effective deterrent in a bear encounter. Learn how to use it and keep it accessible.

➢ If you encounter a bear, stay calm, avoid direct eye contact, and slowly back away. Do not run. If a bear charges, stand your ground and use bear spray if necessary.

➢ Moose: Moose may appear calm but can be aggressive – They are especially dangerous during mating season (fall) and when they have calves (spring).

➢ Allow moose plenty of space - A moose with raised hackles, pinned ears, or licking its lips may charge. If one charges, run behind a tree or other obstacle.

Wolves and Other Predators.

➢ Wolves rarely attack humans, but if you do encounter one, stand your ground, make yourself appear larger, and slowly back away.

➢ To avoid attracting scavengers, keep food and trash stored securely.

➢ Avoid approaching smaller animals, such as porcupines, beavers, and rodents, as they may bite or carry diseases.

➢ Be wary of beaver lodges along waterways; beavers may react aggressively if they feel threatened.

Weather Hazards and How to Be Safe
Alaska's weather can change quickly, bringing high winds, heavy rain, and even snow in the summer months. Cold and hypothermia

➤ Always layer your clothes. Sudden temperature drops can cause hypothermia if you are not prepared. Wear moisture-wicking fabrics and avoid cotton.
➤ Stay dry – Wet clothing and cold winds promote heat loss. Waterproof gear is essential.
➤ Know the symptoms of hypothermia - Shivering, slurred speech, confusion, and lack of coordination are all warning signs. If symptoms appear, get dry, warm up, and seek shelter right away.

Heat & Dehydration
While Alaska is known for its cold weather, summer hikes can still result in dehydration, particularly in exposed tundra or alpine areas.

➤ If you're hiking long distances, drink plenty of water and bring electrolyte supplements.
➤ Fog, Rain, and Snow
➤ Heavy fog can obscure trails and make navigation difficult. Bring a map, compass, or GPS.
➤ Rain can muddy trails and cause rivers to swell dangerously. Check the weather before leaving.
➤ Unexpected snowstorms can occur even in the summer. If you get caught in heavy snowfall, seek shelter and stay put until visibility improves.

Terrain Hazards and Safe Travel Tips:

Alaska's trails vary from well-maintained paths to rugged, off-trail wilderness.

Unstable Ground and Rockfall

➢ Many trails pass through scree fields, loose rock, and eroded cliffs. Before you step, make sure your footing is secure and test the rocks.

➢ Walking directly beneath steep rock faces is not recommended because falling debris poses a significant risk.

River crossings

➢ Glacial rivers can be extremely dangerous due to their fast currents and cold temperatures.

➢ If you must cross a river, look for wide, shallow areas and use trekking poles to maintain balance. Undo your backpack straps so you can easily remove it if you fall in.

➢ Never cross a river barefoot; instead, wear sturdy footwear to keep your feet safe from sharp rocks.

Ice & Glaciers

Never hike on a glacier without the necessary equipment and experience. Crevasses present hidden hazards, and ice can be extremely slippery.

When exploring icefields, work with a guide or use crampons and an ice axe for stability.

11.3. First Aid and Safety Advice for Remote Areas

Alaska's backcountry is vast and frequently remote from medical facilities. Being prepared with first-aid knowledge and supplies can help keep minor injuries from becoming major problems.

Basic first aid kit for Alaska hikers.
- A well-stocked kit should contain:
- Bandages, gauze, and adhesive tape.
- Antiseptic wipes and antibacterial ointment
- Pain relievers (ibuprofen and acetaminophen)
- Tweezers (to remove splinters or ticks).
- Blister treatment (moleskin, blister pads)
- elastic wrap for sprains.
- Emergency blanket
- Prescription medications (as needed)
- Common Hiking Injuries & Treatment
- Blisters
- Wearing well-fitting boots and moisture-wicking socks can help prevent blisters.
- If a blister develops, use moleskin or a bandage to reduce friction.
- Sprains & Strains
- If you twist your ankle, rest, compress, and elevate it.
- Use trekking poles to maintain stability and avoid putting too much weight on the injured area.
- Dehydration and Heat Exhaustion
- Drink plenty of fluids and rest in shaded areas.

➤ If you feel dizzy, nauseated, or weak, rest and hydrate right away.

Hypothermia and frostbite
➤ If someone is shivering uncontrollably or confused, provide them with dry clothing, body heat, and warm liquids.
➤ To treat frostbite, avoid rubbing the skin and instead gradually warm it.
➤ Being prepared for medical emergencies is critical when hiking in Alaska's remote wilderness. Carrying a basic first-aid kit, knowing how to treat common injuries, and knowing when to call for assistance can make a big difference.

Chapter 12

2025 Budget for Your Alaska Trip

Planning a hiking trip to Alaska is an exciting adventure, but you must budget carefully to ensure a smooth and enjoyable experience. Costs can quickly add up, particularly for transportation, lodging, permits, and gear. By planning ahead of time, you can make the most of your trip while staying within your budget.

12.1. Calculating Your Total Trip Costs

The cost of your Alaska hiking trip will vary depending on the time of year, length of stay, and desired level of comfort. Here's a breakdown of potential expenses:

1. Transportation costs.

Flights to Alaska: Round-trip airfare to major cities such as Anchorage or Fairbanks typically costs between $300 and $1,200, depending on your departure location and season. Summer months (June to August) are the most expensive.

Local Transportation:

Rental cars typically cost $60 to $150 per day, plus gas.

Shuttle Services: Prices vary by route but typically range between $30 and $100 per person.

Ferries and Boat Transportation: Ferry tickets for exploring coastal areas can range from $50 to $500, depending on the distance and type of vessel.

Train Travel: The Alaska Railroad provides scenic routes at ticket prices ranging from $60 to $300.

2. Accommodation Costs: Standard hotels range from $150 to $350 per night, while luxury lodges can cost more than $500.

Cabins and Airbnbs: Prices vary greatly, ranging from $100 to $400 per night, depending on location and features.

Campgrounds: Public campgrounds typically cost $10 to $30 per night, whereas private campgrounds can cost $25 to $50 per night.

Backcountry camping is free in most national parks, but some require permits, which cost between $10 and $30 per trip.

3. Food and dining expenses.

Grocery Costs: If you're cooking meals, set aside $10 to $20 per day for groceries.

Casual restaurant meals range from $15 to $30.

Mid-range restaurants charge $30 to $60 per meal.

Fine dining costs $60 to $100+ per meal.

Trail Snacks and Freeze-Dried Meals: Pre-packaged hiking meals cost between $5 and $15 per meal.

4. Gear & Equipment

If you already have hiking gear, your costs will be minimal. However, if you need to buy or rent equipment, consider the following.

Hiking Boots: $100 to $250.

Backpack: $100–$300.

Tent: $100-$400

Sleeping bag costs $100-$300.

Bear Canister (required in many areas): $50-$100 (rentals available for $5-$10 per day)

Trekking poles: $50–$150.

Rain gear costs $50-$200.

Bear Spray: $30–$50.

5. Parking Fees and Permits

National Park Entrance Fees: Most parks charge between $15 and $30 per vehicle. An annual America the Beautiful pass costs $80 and covers all of the United States' national parks.

Backcountry Permits: Certain areas require permits, which can cost anywhere from $10 to $50 per person.

Guided Tours: Prices vary greatly but typically range between $100 and $500 per day, depending on the activity and location.

6. Other costs

Travel insurance is recommended for remote hiking trips. Expect to pay between $50 and $150, depending on coverage.

Satellite Communication Devices: If renting, expect to pay between $10 and $20 per day for devices such as Garmin inReach.

Souvenirs and extras: Budget between $50 and $200 for souvenirs, books, and local crafts.

12.2 Tips for a Budget-Friendly Trip

While Alaska can be expensive, there are ways to save money without sacrificing the experience:

1. Travel during shoulder seasons.

Visiting in May or September allows you to save money on flights, lodging, and car rentals while still enjoying excellent hiking conditions.

2. Take advantage of free or low-cost activities.

Many of Alaska's best hiking trails are free to use, and wildlife viewing does not require a tour.

3. Cook Your Meals.

Grocery shopping and cooking at your campsite or lodge can dramatically reduce food costs.

4. Camp instead of staying in hotels.

Public campgrounds are inexpensive and provide an up-close experience with nature.

5. Rent or Borrow Gear: Rather than purchasing expensive equipment, consider renting from outfitters in Anchorage or Fairbanks.

6. Take public transportation or carpool.

The Alaska Railroad and shuttle services provide scenic transportation for a lower cost than rental cars.

12.3. Sample Budget for Various Travelers

Budget Traveler (7-Day Trip)

Flight costs $400 (off-season).

Camping costs $10 per night ($70 total).

Food (grocery and snacks): $100

Park fees are $30.

Rental car (shared with others): $200. Total cost: $800–$1,200.

Mid-Range Traveler (7-Day Trip)
Flight costs $600.
Lodging (hotels and cabins): $1,200.
Food (a combination of restaurants and groceries): $300
Park fees and permits cost $50.
The rental car costs $400.
Guided activity (e.g., whale watching or glacier tour) costs $200, totaling $2,500–$3,000.

Luxury Traveler (7-Day Trip)
Flight costs $1,000 (peak season, first class).
Lodging (luxury lodge or resort) costs $3,000
Dining at high-end restaurants costs $800
Private guided hikes and tours cost $1,500.
A rental car with extras costs $600, totaling $6,000+.

Made in the USA
Middletown, DE
05 June 2025

76612121R00080